The New
Geopolitics
of Energy

During the financial year 1996/7 the Energy and Environmental Programme is supported by generous contributions of finance and technical advice from the following organizations:

Ashland Oil • British Gas • British Nuclear Fuels • British Petroleum
Brown and Root • Department of Trade and Industry • Eastern Electricity
Enron • Enterprise Oil • Esso/Exxon • LASMO • Magnox Electric
Mitsubishi Fuels • National Grid • Nuclear Electric • PowerGen • Ruhrgas
St Clements Services • Saudi Aramco • Shell • Statoil • TEPCO • Texaco
Veba Oil

Additional support is received for specific research projects from the following:

ABB • Chubu Electric Power Co • Commission of the European Communities
Department of Environment UK • East Asia Gas Company • ENEL
Hydro-Quebec • Imatran Voima Oy • Japan National Oil Company
London Electricity • Ministry of Foreign Affairs, Norway • Ministry of
Industry and Energy, Norway • Palmco • Siemens • Tennessee Valley
Authority • UK Foreign and Commonwealth Office

Additional funding for specific meetings and workshops has been received from:

Amerada Hess • Australian Environment Agency • Environment Agency,
Japan • GISPRI • Greenpeace • International Climate Change Partnership
Mobil • Rolls Royce Industrial Power • RTZ-CRA Group • Swiss
Environment Ministry • Uranium Institute • US State Department.

The New Geopolitics of Energy

John Mitchell
with Peter Beck
and Michael Grubb

THE ROYAL INSTITUTE OF
INTERNATIONAL AFFAIRS
Energy and Environmental Programme

First published in Great Britain in 1996 by

Royal Institute of International Affairs, 10 St James's Square, London SW1Y 4LE
(Charity Registration No. 208 223)

Distributed exclusively by
The Brookings Institution, 1775 Massachusetts Avenue NW,
Washington DC 20036-2188

ISBN 1 899658 12 2

Printed and bound by Redwood Books Limited, Trowbridge, Wilts.
Cover by Harry Brockway.

THIS BOOK IS DEDICATED
TO THE MEMORY OF

ROBERT BELGRAVE

founder of the Energy and Environmental
Programme at the RIIA, sometime director of
BP International and sometime member of the
UK diplomatic service

*HIS WISDOM WAS ALWAYS TO
CHALLENGE THE CONVENTIONAL*

Contents

Abbreviations

AIOC	Azerbaijan International Oil Consortium
APEC	Asia-Pacific Economic Cooperation
ASEAN	Association of Southeast Asian Nations
bn bbl	billion barrels (one thousand million)
CERI	Canadian Energy Research Institute
CIS	Commonwealth of Independent States
ESCAP	Economic Commission for Asia and the Pacific
EEA	European Economic Area
EIA	Energy Information Administration
FBR	fast breeder reactor
FNR	fast neutron reactor
FSU	Former Soviet Union
GATT	General Agreement on Tariffs and Trade
IAEA	International Atomic Energy Agency
IEA	International Energy Agency
IFP	Institut Français du Pétrole
IISASA	International Institute of Applied Systems Analysis
IPCC	Intergovernmental Panel on Climate Change
JI	joint implementation
JNOC	Japan National Oil Company
kgoe	kilogram of oil equivalent
LNG	liquefied natural gas
LWR	light water reactor
MITI	Ministry of International Trade and Industry (Japan)
mmtoe	million tonnes of oil equivalent
mmbd	million barrels per day
MOX	mixed oxide fuel
mta	thousand tonnes annually
OECD	Organization for Economic Cooperation and Development
OPEC	Organization of Petroleum Exporting Countries
NPT	Non-Proliferation Treaty
NNPA	Nuclear Non-Proliferation Act
R/P	reserve to production ratios
START	Strategic Arms Reduction Treaty
SPR	strategic petroleum reserve
TWh	terawatt hours (one thousand billion)

Foreword

This study grew out of the authors' conviction that debates about the international politics of energy depend too much on ideas drawn from the conflicts of the 1970s. The oil crises, the 'OPEC Cartel', 'Energy dependence' and the like were set in the international context which preceded the end of the Cold War, the break-up of the Soviet Union, the development of the Middle East peace process, and the commitment of China to economic reform. In the narrower world of energy also, much has changed since the fall in oil prices of 1983–6.

The purpose of this work is to take stock, to evaluate the changes, and to propose a new calculus for the international energy debate. The result has been to define an international – or geopolitical – dimension to energy policy which is mainly concerned with supply, not in the sense of imminent shortages but in terms of a struggle for advantage.

Geopolitical concerns are not necessarily contradictory to the environmental concerns which bear mainly on demand and which have been a driving force in national energy policies in recent years. One demand-oriented environmental policy is inevitably international – climate change policy. But the geopolitics of supply are still there, though they have changed. Their existence means that energy policies, constructed in a modern idiom, cannot be regarded simply as the dirty linen of environmental policies; it is indeed the interaction of all these factors that is a hallmark of the new geopolitics.

The Energy and Environmental Programme of the Royal Institute of International Affairs (Chatham House) is uniquely placed to conduct a study of these changes and their interactions. The Programme has a wealth of expertise in both established energy geopolitics and a proven track record in many of the new supply and environmental dimensions. John Mitchell, Chairman of the Programme, deserves particular recognition for his outstanding work in leading the research and associated activities that have produced this book, including writing most of the material presented here except Chapters 6 and 7.

The core research was sponsored by Statoil in preparation for a workshop organized with the RIIA in Oslo on 11–12 April 1996. Heads of no less than four of RIIA's research programmes – Rosemary Hollis, Roy Allison, Richard Grant, and Michael Grubb – contributed to the seminar, reflecting the strength and diversity of the Institute's expertise on geopolitical issues. Support from the UK Foreign and Commonwealth Office has enabled the work to be expanded further and published as this full-length book. Some of the material in Chapters 2–5 appeared in a briefing paper prepared by John Mitchell under the sponsorship of the European Commission's Energy Directorate for their Workshop 'Energy 2020' in Brussels on 19-20 June 1995. The financial support of all these bodies is gratefully acknowledged.

October 1996   Professor J.E. Spence
Director of Studies, RIIA

Acknowledgments

Apart from acknowledging the generous financial support for this project mentioned in the Foreword, we would like to express our thanks to those who took part in the various workshops at which these subjects were discussed, which contributed to our thinking. The Oslo workshop was particularly helpful in shaping the final conclusions. We are grateful also to Denny Ellerman, Sydney Freemantle, David Jenkins, Yasuko Kawashima, Hoesung Lee, Peter Odell, Hermann Ott, Toufiq Siddiqi, Helga Steeg, Jonathan Stern, Steve Thomas and Tsutomo Toichi, who read drafts of the text or specific chapters and provided useful comments. Matthew Tickle, EEP's Programme Manager, displayed his usual efficiency and good humour in managing the process and compiling the medley of text and figures into a single document.

The opinions expressed, and any errors and omissions, are entirely the responsibility of the authors. The controversial nature of some of the arguments in the report means that the usual disclaimers apply with full force.

October 1996   John Mitchell
Michael Grubb
Peter Beck

Executive summary

Energy has lost the priority on the geopolitical agenda that it gained from the idea of an 'energy crisis'. Energy policy on the supply side is now generally secondary to geopolitical issues of foreign policy and security; energy demand policies are mainly driven by environmental objectives; and governments almost everywhere have given way to markets for allocating investment and trade.

Oil production outside OPEC, and outside the Middle East, is likely to continue to rise until 2010 so that the share of OPEC and Middle Eastern supplies in the world oil market may not increase.

Oil prices are unlikely to show a long term trend before 2010 but may rise or fall during investment cycles and short-term market disruptions. The prospect of a long-term aggressive oil price cartel is remote.

In the Middle East, geopolitical rivalry between the principal petroleum exporters will reinforce commercial competition to expand production capacity and export revenues. In some countries revenue expansion is unlikely in the near and medium term. The contrast between static revenues and increasing needs will strain their political stability and their ability to protect the buying of arms.

Iran's and Iraq's relations with the rest of the world are very difficult, compared to those of Saudi Arabia (which now supplies half the Middle East's oil). Conflicts between countries, combined with internal strain, increase the risk that local political events will temporarily disrupt oil supplies.

Russia remains a petroleum superpower. Enterprises in the oil sector increasingly operate as part of the world oil industry. However, Gazprom, the largest hydrocarbon producer in the world, remains a monopoly in Russia. Russian gas is set to grow in importance in the European gas market. This depends on wider economic and political relationships between Russia and countries in the rest of Europe, whatever their relationship with one another and with the USA.

The political relations between Russia and its southern neighbours are critical to the development of the hydrocarbon resources of the Caspian sea for export.

Rapid economic growth in East Asia is changing the balance of world energy markets: the region already consumes more energy than Europe and as much as the USA. The major options for securing the expansion and diversification of energy supplies depend on international cooperation: to resolve boundary disputes affecting unexplored oil provinces; to provide a framework for investment in cross-border projects for new supplies of gas, either from new liquefied natural gas (LNG) sources or from eastern Russia; and to expand nuclear power in some countries.

Nuclear power has elsewhere become the object of geopolitical and security and environmental fears rather than energy hope. Managing these fears requires international cooperation on trade in plutonium, spent fuel, and technology. Restoring the hope requires more R&D than the private sector, or any one country, is likely to provide.

The politics of climate change mitigation are likely to alter the distribution of future energy demand between regions and fuels in the long run. Negotiations about how commitments are to be shared and implemented over time engage geopolitical as well as energy and economic factors which will increase in importance.

Energy ministries and their policies everywhere have a role in relating geopolitical objectives to the realities of energy markets and local environmental objectives for the clean use of energy.

The USA has a role in every issue on the agenda of the new geopolitics of energy. Other governments have decisive roles in relation to particular issues. Coordination of international actions in the many different forums involved is critical to progress.

The 'new geopolitics', in contrast to the old, is creative rather than defensive, aligned to market-orientated development rather than state management. There are prizes to be shared for successful international cooperation:

- to promote stable conditions for the flow of cross-border investment and technology;
- to broaden participation in arrangements to alleviate temporary disruptions of energy supply;
- to establish stable conditions for Russian gas and oil exports to Europe and for the development and export of Caspian oil and gas;
- to provide a framework for investment to expand gas supplies to East Asia;
- to develop more widely acceptable options for nuclear power;
- to agree and implement shared policies to mitigate the risk of climate change.

Chapter 1

Introduction and overview

This book is about how changes in the scale and structure of energy demand, supply and international trade have become interwoven with broader, non-energy political changes. We argue that for the next fifteen or more years the arithmetic of the energy outlook and current international political trends create a new 'geopolitics of energy' which differs greatly from the OECD–OPEC focus of earlier decades.

The book is mostly about energy supply, because that is most subject to geopolitics. The exception is the issue of global climate change, which is potentially interwoven in all of these dimensions and is considered in Chapter 7.

This is not an encyclopaedia of energy: hydro and renewable energies, which are of growing importance in many countries but have a limited geopolitical dimension, are mentioned only in connection with the global issue of climate change policy. This book focuses mainly on petroleum, and the rise of natural gas, because the international dimension of these fuels is so pervasive, but the international issues affecting nuclear energy are discussed in Chapter 6: these too have changed.

The geographical coverage is selective: except for their contribution to world oil supply and demand there is little about Latin America or South Asia and nothing about Africa, though in each region there are cross-border issues which are of importance in the politics and energy trade of the region. Nor is this a history of energy policy, though there are some comments in the concluding chapter on the implications of the 'new geopolitics' for national energy policies and international discussions of energy issues.

What is new

What is new in the mix of energy and international politics can be summarized as follows:

- Oil's place in the energy mix has fallen; its price is below the level preceding the 1979 oil shock; there is no perception of near- or medium-term 'shortage'; the share of the Middle East in the oil mix has fallen; the relative position of the main Middle East oil exporters has changed in favour of Saudi Arabia. The oil market has become more open, competitive and transparent – a commodity market with the trading instruments common in such markets for futures and hedging operations.

- The end of the Cold War has removed a major constraint on the freedom of US action in the Middle East and in other parts of the world. The United States has demonstrated its military power on the ground in the Middle East to protect, among other things, an important part of that region's oil supplies to the world market. In 1996, as the book goes to press, the USA (alone or in concert with others) maintains sanctions against the development of oil production and in some cases exports from three major exporters: Iraq, Iran and Libya.

- Immense and comprehensive changes are integrating Russia and other former members of the Soviet Union into the world economy, their energy sectors included, with effects which are different for oil than for gas. Relations between Russia and the other successor states (and former USSR allies) have changed and are still developing, with consequences for the flow of energy trade across new and old borders.

- Gas is growing in importance relative to oil, led by a combination of technical and regulatory changes in the electricity sector. Especially in and around Europe, but also more widely, the international politics of gas investment and trade are becoming as complex and potentially as important as, but increasingly distinct from, those of oil.

- Asia could well become the most active theatre for the 'new geopolitics' of energy. Economic growth in East Asia, including economic reform in China, has put that region's energy consumption ahead of Europe's and it is overtaking that of the USA. At the same time, China is increasing its international reach and the relationship between Russia and the region is becoming more flexible following the end of the Cold War.

- Nuclear energy in much of the developed world has changed from the subject of hope to the object of fear; hope, and ambitious plans for nuclear expansion, still prevail in most of the Asian developing countries, while in the countries where nuclear power originated there is increasing concern about the risks for long-term containment of spent nuclear fuel.

- A global political process to mitigate human contributions to climate change has begun. In the long run this may profoundly alter the rate of growth of energy demand and shift it away from fuels which emit greenhouse gases.

- The probability of disruptions of supply, or of investment, in the Middle East, is not new. But the risk is probably growing, as the economic tensions among (and within) the oil exporting countries become more severe. Management of disruption remains an international policy question, even though 'confronting the cartel' has disappeared from the agenda as the limits to the price-setting potential of OPEC have become clear, even to its former adversaries.

The energy calculations

Although this book does not present detailed scenarios, some numbers matter:

- Oil production outside OPEC and the former Soviet Union may well continue to increase to 2010 at the same rate as it has in the past. Combined with the eventual resumption of growth in Russian production, the result would be that for most conventional projections of oil demand the OPEC share of supply would not grow and the call on the Middle East in particular would remain around 30%; to 2000 the call may not grow significantly even in absolute volume (see Chapter 2 and especially Figure 2.5).

- The Saudi share of Middle East production is unlikely to fall from around 45%. In the long run, competition to expand capacity will be intense. Order in the expansion of capacity and the management of short-run surpluses will depend on Saudi Arabia's influence as the dominant supplier (see Chapter 3 and especially Figure 3.7).

- Russia is a petroleum superpower. Gazprom, currently the largest hydrocarbon producer in the world, will lead an expansion of gas exports to Europe more or less at the rate and on the terms which it and the Russian government choose (See Chapter 4 and especially Figure 4.4). Production of oil could grow to 7–8 mmbd by 2010. Privatized Russian companies will compete to bring this production to the export market.

- East Asia will soon overtake the USA as a market for energy. Energy intensity trends in East Asia are no different from those elsewhere. Though the precise level of demand by 2010 has wide uncertainties there will certainly be a demand for growing imports which governments will support rather than risk damage to economic growth. To meet this demand there will be a shift from the present dominance of coal and oil in the region as a whole towards more use of natural gas and non-fossil fuels, particularly nuclear and hydro power. To supply natural gas, eastern Russia will be a strong competitor if the political environment for pipeline projects can be created (see Chapter 5 and especially Figures 5.5 and 5.9).

- Nuclear energy is set to grow in parts of the developing world, especially East Asia, where electricity demand is rising rapidly and capital may well be available. However, there is the chance that the West, headed by the USA, may impede trade in technology in order to limit the trade in plutonium-containing fuel for civil use, a potential weapons proliferation risk. In most of the rest of the world the challenge to the industry is how to escape from the dilemma of being too uneconomic and too suspect in the public's eyes to expand, but too essential in many countries to close plant, with too many safety and security issues unresolved. This challenge might be softened by the development of a new generation of safer and more economic reactors, with a fuel cycle less prone to proliferation concerns. This would require international collaboration and funding (see Chapter 6).

- Renewable energy, from non-traditional sources, has begun to appear on forecasters' screens as a portfolio of supply options – biomass, solar, wind – which in the long term could decouple the growth of energy consumption from the growth in carbon dioxide emissions. Chapter 7 describes the policy process which could reinforce this trend.

The policy agenda

The geopolitical agenda affecting these energy calculations is broad: much of it is outside the reach of the governments of OECD or OPEC countries. There is some feedback from the energy arithmetic to broader geopolitical issues and relationships. Chapter 8 identifies issues where the most economic energy solutions appear to require broad international cooperation, and where achieving such cooperation on the energy issues would be an important contribution to a wider agenda of reducing international conflict and increasing cooperation.

These issues are:

- managing responses to future disruptions to international energy trade: oil supply to the world market and gas supply to Europe in particular;
- resolving tensions inhibiting the development of oil and gas exports from the former Soviet Union;
- improving the environment for investment in projects and pipelines to export gas from eastern Russia to Northeast Asia;
- broadening the basis for policy commitments and actions to reduce greenhouse gas emissions with global effect;
- finding cooperative mechanisms for developing and gaining wider acceptance for safer and more economical nuclear options.

Each of these issues has a different international constituency: different forums and processes are relevant in each case. Many governments now leave markets to balance supply and demand and carry out investments in energy. There is also a different weight of private-sector and public policy decision makers according to the issue and the countries concerned. In East Asia, most governments still play a strong role. The USA has a distinct role, and defined objectives, on every issue. In Europe the complexities of policy-making in the European Union make initiatives difficult. Everywhere, the geopolitical issues of energy must be reconciled with broader policy agendas of competitiveness, foreign policy and environmental policy. Specialist energy ministries and departments may have a central and integrative role in this reconciliation, but they will get little help from the old, narrowly cast headings of old 'energy policies': they need the 'new geopolitics'.

Chapter 2

The oil machine (non-OPEC oil)

Introduction

This chapter describes some features of world oil supply and outlook
which were not obvious ten or twenty years ago:

- The international oil market has 'globalized'. International prices reach
  most producers and consumers, modified only by taxes. International
  trade is based on formal and informal open and relatively transparent
  commodity markets.
- Production outside OPEC, and outside the former Soviet Union/CIS,
  has grown very steadily, despite wide variations in price.
- For the next fifteen years, perhaps longer, this steady growth is likely to
  continue, given continuation of policies in these producing countries.
- Production in the former Soviet Union/CIS (for reasons explained further in Chapter 4) is also likely to resume growth.
- The result is that, contrary to some recent forecasts, the OPEC share of
  world oil production is unlikely to grow rapidly before 2010 – in fact it
  may remain stable or even drop temporarily.
- For the Middle East, the numbers are slightly smaller than for OPEC,
  but the trend in production share is similar.

The consequence of this analysis is that there is no geographic reason
why oil supplies should be more prone to cartelization than they have been
in the past ten years (OPEC share of world production rose from 30% in
1985 to 41% in 1994; it had been 51% in 1973). Disruption is another
question, which is discussed in the next chapter.

Trade and market structure

The development of the global market in crude oil has been extensively described and analysed.[1] This market has developed in a geopolitical environment in which the governments of major oil-importing and consuming countries, and of many oil producers (including Russia since 1993) have generally reduced their attempts to manage economic matters, including trade and prices, across a wide range of subjects, including energy. Information and communications technology has facilitated instant communication of pricing information and contract offers and acceptances across the world's trading screens. The expertise of other commodity markets, including financial and exchange markets, has been brought to the oil trade.

The open international commodity market for oil was not only driven by developments in the importing countries. It would not have advanced so rapidly if many OPEC governments had not destroyed the trading channels which previously existed within a few major international integrated companies. During the 1970s, most OPEC governments nationalized or took over by 'participation' the upstream operations in their territories of integrated international private-sector companies and then during the second oil shock destroyed the 'long-term contracts' which maintained special relationships with those companies.[2]

As a result of these two developments – marketization and deregulation in much of the world, and de-integration of most OPEC oil exports – the international oil market is the central feature of the relationship between producers and consumers in the 'new geopolitics'. Ideas of a producer–consumer dialogue at government level, or special favourable bilateral relationships between individual producer and consumer countries, are inevitably marginalized when on the consumer side markets are open, the state has withdrawn and competition prevails.[3]

---

[1]   See, for example Hartshorn (1993); Horsnell and Mabro (1993); and Horsnell (1996).

[2]   The UK experiment of 'painless participation', which created the British National Oil Company as a state-controlled trading vehicle, was terminated in 1979 following the election of Mrs Thatcher's government.

[3]   Ironically, in the new geopolitics, driven by non-energy factors, there is a place for *negative* special relationships, as demonstrated by the US sanctions on Iran and Libya.

Figure 2.1 Actual oil production by region 1965–95

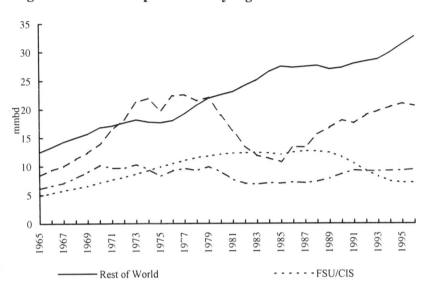

———— Rest of World   · · · · · · FSU/CIS

— · — · OPEC outside Middle East   — — — Middle East

Source: *BP Statistical Review* (1995).

Non-OPEC production

Future non-OPEC supplies have often been underestimated,[4] except in the United States, where future US output has often been overestimated. With hindsight, it looks as though forecasters frequently overstated the effect of depletion and of prices on supply, and did not allow adequately for the effects of technology on recovery rates and the economics of developing small pools, and of policies of leasing and taxation in mitigating the fluctuations of price.

Oil production in the former Soviet Union/CIS expanded extraordinarily fast, by more than 5 mmbd, between 1965 and 1976, and collapsed extraordinarily fast, by 6 mmbd, between 1989 and 1994. The reasons are discussed elsewhere in this paper. The exclusion of the FSU/CIS from

---

[4] For a review of some forecasting errors, see Lynch (1995). An early challenge to conventional wisdom was Odell (1980).

Figure 2.2 Share of world oil production by region 1965–1996

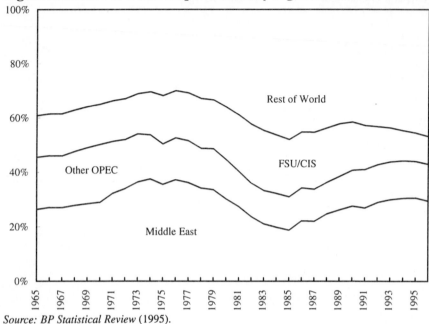

Source: BP Statistical Review (1995).

'Non-OPEC' numbers reveals a very steady trend, as Figure 2.1 shows. In fact, oil production in the 'rest of the world' – outside the Middle East, the rest of OPEC and the former Soviet Union – has grown remarkably steadily over thirty years, from 12 mmbd (600 mmta) in 1965 to almost 34 mmbd (1,693 mmta) in 1995, with only three years in which growth was interrupted. This contrasted with the surges in OPEC and FSU/CIS production and was not reversed by the fall in oil prices. Annual increases in the 'rest of the world' over 1965-95 averaged about 0.6 mmbd, only twice exceeding 1 mmbd. Decreases did not exceed 0.5 mmbd in any year. Development of production in this area is subject to a more complex process than either simple depletion or simple elasticity to supply prices.[5]

While production outside OPEC has grown steadily, and Russian production has fluctuated more or less with local demand (see Chapter 4), OPEC production has absorbed most of the remaining fluctuations in

---

[5]   A simple conceptual model is proposed in Mitchell (1994b).

world oil demand. The effect on the relative shares of the producing regions is shown Figure 2.2. If the Middle East (OPEC and non-OPEC) is separated from the other groups its share of production in 1995 was 30%, compared with that of OPEC at 40%.

Reasons for continuing growth in oil production outside OPEC and the former Soviet Union

Market orientation

In 1979 US oil price controls were eliminated; Canada followed suit soon thereafter. In the USA, Canada, the UK and Norway during the 1980s and early 1990s tax regimes were changed, removed or reduced. The Windfall Profits tax in the USA and the Special Petroleum duty in the UK were eliminated. In the UK, petroleum revenue tax rates were reduced, and new developments were relieved of petroleum revenue tax and royalty. In a number of developing countries production-sharing terms followed a similar trend. In the UK and Canada state oil enterprises (BNOC and Petrocanada) were dismantled or privatized, as was YPF in Argentina.

Policies of increasing access and openness were also important. In the USA, access policies have been important, but negative. Since 1989, moratoriums on exploration and/or development have applied for environmental reasons to the east and west coasts offshore, the Alaskan National Wildlife Reserve, and coastal wetlands. Perhaps as much as 30 billion barrels of potential reserves have been withheld from development.

Elsewhere, the story has been of increasing access to the international private-sector industry. A number of developing countries reduced the areas reserved for state monopolies and offered new territory to joint venturing or production-sharing by the international industry: Egypt, Syria, Yemen, India, Pakistan, China, Thailand, Vietnam, the Philippines, Cuba, Ecuador, Peru and Colombia are the principal examples.

There are still areas where domestic political conditions or unattractive terms have so far prevented significant foreign private or domestic state exploration and development, such as Myanmar, Mozambique and Zaire, or where exploration and development is impeded by territorial dispute – the Spratly Islands and the South Atlantic are examples.

Commercialization of state companies

Complete domination of the oil industry by the state is becoming uncommon outside OPEC. Norway has always been an exception in which a major role for the state company – automatically sharing in 51% of new discoveries – was made compatible with private sector participation. From 1996 this privilege will cease for further new discoveries as Norway complies with European Economic Area (EEA) obligations on national treatment for foreign firms. There may eventually be changes in Brazil and Mexico, where development slowed in the early 1990s. The key policy decisions which favoured development there in the early 1980s had been for the governments to finance aggressive investment by the state oil companies. In Mexico this policy ground to a halt after the Mexican debt crisis of 1986. Steps were taken in 1994 to 'corporatize' Pemex so as to stimulate as far as possible the management's approach to costs and commercial behaviour, but the state's monopoly of hydrocarbon reserves and development was excluded from the North American Free Trade negotiations and has been confirmed by the current administration.[6] In Brazil, Petrobras found it difficult to sustain investment during the government's financial crises of 1993-5. The constitutional barrier to foreign participation in Petrobras' developments was lifted in 1995.

Technology and innovation

Within the private sector, tax systems which allow enterprises to share the benefits of successful exploration and cost saving provide a powerful incentive to innovation, both technical and managerial. There is no reason to suppose that this process has stopped or is slowing down. State companies, such as Pemex and Petrobras, are increasingly being subject to pseudo-commercial accountability in an attempt to simulate these incentives.

Development reflects technology in two ways. First, as new oil provinces are discovered (e.g. offshore Europe, Brazil, and Mexico) new technology steadily reduces the cost of exploration and development: in exploration through 3D and '4D' seismic computer modelling of entire

---

[6]   Address by President Zedillo at Chatham House, 30 January 1996.

basins, and the integration of geology, geophysics and geochemistry; in drilling, through extended reach and horizontal drilling; in production, by multiple completion and computer-aided reservoir management plans and monitoring; in engineering, through reduction of platform weight, new integrated design concepts, and subsea completion techniques. Second, the same technical factors enhance production from mature areas by increasing recovery rates and enabling the development of satellite reservoirs previously regarded as uneconomic.[7] The private-sector oil industry has achieved remarkable reductions in costs and lead times.[8]

Cost reductions

In the USA, finding costs appear to have fallen from $16 per barrel in 1983 to around $4.50 per barrel in 1994. US companies' finding costs outside the USA fell from $9–10 to around $5 per barrel over the same period.[9] Although there were technology-based savings in drilling involved, the changes also probably reflect the improved selection of drilling targets – partly due to improved seismic technology, partly to more rigorous commercial criteria: poor prospects were not pursued. However, the US Department of Energy in 1994 estimated the economically recoverable reserves of the USA in 2010 to be higher than was estimated in 1990 by 41% (gas) and 37% (oil) as a result of technological innovation. US companies at the beginning of the 1990s reduced their upstream capital expenditure on oil (and gas) in the USA in favour of activity in other countries where opportunities were being opened up. This trend appears to have halted. The convergence of US and non-US finding costs may be a sign of the final globalization of the private-sector industry: investment is directed to the lowest-cost areas available. The (US) waters of the Gulf of Mexico are competitive with the widening foreign opportunities.

In the UK, traditionally perceived as a 'high cost' producer, the story has been of dramatic reductions in development costs for new fields, from

---

[7] See Appert (1985).

[8] See the short overview in Davies (1995).

[9] US Department of Energy (1996).

Figure 2.3 Oil production by country outside OPEC and the FSU/CIS, 1965–94

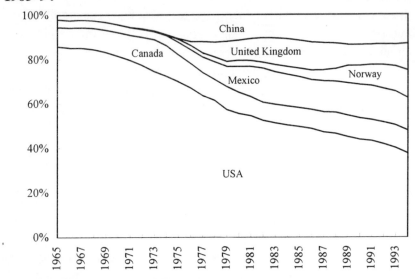

Source: *BP Statistical Review* (1995).

around $14 capital expenditure per barrel in the early 1980s to around $12 per barrel for fields being developed in 1993. Even lower numbers are now reported. Producers' innovation sustains discovery and development. 'Growth' of identified reserves, due to innovation and cost saving, has been the main source of reserve growth for the past decade. The effect of all these developments on one province – the North Sea – has been detailed in a recent IEA study.[10]

Geographical diversification

Figure 2.3 shows that the combination of environmentally motivated restrictions offshore and wetlands exploration in the USA, with new areas opening elsewhere (with the benefit of technological improvement) has steadily diversified the growing 'rest of the world' supply. The steady opening of new

---

[10] IEA (1995d).

oil areas to commercial development has enabled production from these areas to make good the decline in US production, and has also greatly diversified the sources of supply. In 1965, the USA provided two-thirds of production outside OPEC, the Middle East and the former Soviet Union. As Figure 2.3 shows, by 1994 the US share had fallen to one-third.

Potential for future production

The foregoing analysis suggests that there are important differences between the production records of the four principal groups of countries. Some of these differences may be due to different access to technology, different regimes for licensing and access, different tax regimes and (at times) isolation from international prices. In the case of OPEC the key difference has been the willingness or desire of the producing countries to withhold production from existing capacity in order to support the price. Except possibly in the case of the 'lower 48' states of the USA (i.e. excluding Alaska), depletion of oil reserves has not been a constraint. In projecting the possibilities for future production for the next 15 to 20 years, the first question is whether depletion will be a factor limiting either total supply or supplies from particular places.

Some basic dynamics

Estimating the size of existing oil reserves, the proportion of the oil in place in those which will be recovered, and the scale of future additions to oil reserves is difficult and complex: in addition to limitations of physical information, future technology and economics constrain the policy and commercial decisions necessary to 'prove' the reserves and develop production capacity.

Production from any single developed but defined pool of oil will inevitably decline to the point at which the cost of further production becomes uneconomic: oil production 'runs down' rather than 'runs out'. The decline may be offset, or even temporarily reversed, if the rate of recovery is increased by new investment when new technology makes such investment economic. Increased recovery rates – to 50% or more –

have been an important reason for maintaining production in the UK offshore. Worldwide average recovery rates are nearer 35%. It is the objective of the offshore technology industry to develop cost-effective methods
for raising that rate to 50%.[11] As recovery rates rise, estimates of existing
reserves are revised upwards. They may also be revised upwards as
increasing information reveals the existence of connected or adjacent
pools of oil, and the possibility of these being developed with existing
infrastructure is also a source of additions to the economically recoverable
reserves which are represented under various definitions such as 'Proved
Reserves' or 'Identified Reserves'.[12]

New discoveries are a further source of new reserves. These are also difficult to predict. There is no disagreement that the average size of discoveries worldwide has been falling recently, and large discoveries are becoming rare in mature oil provinces. Estimates can be made on the basis of
geological information. The most comprehensive publicly accessible
source of such estimates is that published by the US Geological Survey for
successive World Petroleum Congresses.[13] Statistical methods for extrap-
olating discoveries have been also been developed.[14] However, the ten-
dency has been for statistical estimates to be revised upwards.

For a particular oil province, or even for a long-exploited area such as
the onshore regions of the 'lower 48' states of the USA, production eventually outruns the growth in reserves due to revisions and discoveries: a
technically and commercially 'working inventory' equivalent to about 10
years of current production is maintained by steadily reducing the rate of
production. There will continue to be '10 years' supply' of an ever-
decreasing rate of production.

For most of the world, however, the ratio of reserves to current rates

---

[11] Euan Baird, Chairman of Schlumberger, reported in the *Financial Times*, 10 April 1996.
The key concept is information and control technology which will enable the producer to
monitor and control in real time all the processes that go on in the reservoir during production.
[12] For a discussion of these definitions and concepts, see Masters (1994) and Barnes
(1995).
[13] Masters (1994).
[14] Laherre, Perrodon and Demaison (1994).

of production is much higher than 10: in such places, the excess reserves operate like a manufacturer's excess stock: their value depends upon production at a future date and can be enhanced if current production can be increased.[15]

Ratios of identified reserves to production around 10 are consistent with declining, constant or increasing production, depending on the rate of future discoveries (and reserve growth and additions due to higher recovery rates).

Policy implications

For all their limitations, estimates of reserves and of future discoveries, and their ratios to current production (R/P ratios), provide certain signals for the policy analyst. Ratios of identified reserves to production above 10 signal the possibility of increasing production without further discoveries. In such cases, ratios of total (identified plus future possible discoveries) to current production indicate that decline may be avoided or growth in production may continue – depending on the size of the undiscovered potential and the speed with which it is realized (this is turn is a function of policies of access to the potential area and the relevant economics and technology). Most OPEC state oil producers are in this position. (For them competition depends on the construction of production capacity, as Chapter 4 explains.)

Competition plays an important part in the process. Owners (states or companies) of individual pools of oil with R/P ratios approaching 10 have a strong incentive to innovate in increasing recovery of identified oil and to discover new reserves. If they fail, they their enterprise will shrink; if they are very successful, they may increase their share of the oil market and the value of their enterprise will grow. Most private-sector oil companies are in this position. Policies which promote international private-sector competition and access to identified and potential oil will tend to promote the growth of reserves and the diversification of future oil supply. Policies which restrict such competition will have the opposite effect.

---

[15] The extensive economics literature of the 1970s and 1980s on exhaustible resources centred on this relationship.

Table 2.1 Reserves and production estimates

	Identified bn bbls	Possible total bn bbls	R/P ratio identified	R/P ratio possible total
CIS/FSU	125.1	225.1	43	78
OPEC outside Middle East	123.4	158.5	42	54
Middle East	597.2	714.6	89	106
Rest of World	257.5	475.7	23	42
World	1,103.2	1,573.9	46	66

Sources: Masters (1994) and IEA (1996).

With this simple perspective the possible future of production outside OPEC and the CIS may be put in context. Table 2.1 is extracted from the reserve estimates of Masters (1994) and the production estimates of the IEA.[16] The groupings of countries are discussed below.

The 'Rest of World' countries (neither OPEC nor CIS)

Some 23% of the world's identified oil reserves probably lie outside the Middle East, the rest of OPEC and the CIS. Even in the 'mature' producing areas, proven reserves have grown as a result of technical and cost-saving developments as well as continuing discoveries. Far from 'running out', proved[17] reserves in the 'Rest of World' have tripled over 20 years even while production has steadily increased.[18] The ratio of 23 years of identified reserves to annual production in 'Rest of World' was higher at the end of 1993 than at the end of 1973. Production in the area

---

[16] Masters (1994). The 'possible total' is the sum of the identified (unproduced) reserves and the modal estimate of undiscovered oil. The original paper shows the range of uncertainty on the 'undiscovered' estimates and discusses qualifications to 'identified' estimates. These estimates are used in preference to the *BP Statistical Review* or *Oil and Gas Journal* estimates, which are based on collations of published information because, unlike them, Masters shows estimates for undiscovered oil. The production figures are from the IEA *Oil Market Report 5*, April 1996. IEA data are used because, unlike the *BP Statistical Review*, they exclude natural gas liquids which are not included in Masters' reserve figures.

[17] Using BP definitions and data. The same time series is not available for Masters.

[18] US 'identified' reserves estimated in Masters' papers to the 13th and 14th World Petroleum Congresses, respectively, increased by 5.7 bn bbls between 1 January 1990 and 1 January 1993, while for 'Rest of World' as a whole remaining reserves grew by 13%.

as a whole can expand for many years without new discoveries.

The area is not mature in terms of discovery. If likely discoveries are taken into account, 'Rest of World' contains 30% of the world's probable and possible undiscovered reserves combined, with a ratio of total possible reserves to production of 42.

Reserves in 'Rest of World' have grown in proportion to production for good economic reasons. The underlying mechanism has been well explained by Adelman (1993): in a mature region where most acreage has already been allocated to owners, there is no economic reason to spend money to build reserves much faster than they are likely to be required – the lead time of development. Optimal R/P ratios need not exceed the lead time of development investments. However, individual owners (state- or private-sector) may face depletion in their particular pools. When new acreage is opened to exploration, therefore, there is competition between companies to secure a share of new provinces. For those who are successful reserves will surge ahead of production, generating high R/P ratios for individual enterprises in the new areas when the first discoveries are made and while the development investment is under way. In the case of the Middle East in the 1950s, the discoveries by the companies were so huge as to create an overhang of reserves, and a 'supply push' to develop them, which the state companies acquired when the properties were nationalized in the 1970s. The same pattern can occur for state companies when new provinces are opened as a result of new technology: for example offshore Mexico and Brazil in the 1970s. There is a clear connection between competition and the expansion of reserves and therefore production capacity. This was not much represented in the old, introverted geopolitics of 'security of supply'. It fits well in the new geopolitics alongside the macroeconomic themes of international trade and investment, deregulation of markets, privatization of resources industries and utilities, and competition.

CIS and former Soviet Union

The CIS/FSU contains around 11% of the identified and 21% of the undiscovered oil reserves estimated by Masters, giving 14% of the world total possible oil reserves. Production has fallen in recent years because of lack of investment. With an identified R/P ratio of 43, the area as a whole clearly has scope for continuing increase of production from identified reserves, though individual (now privatized) enterprises may be more interested in exploration. For foreign companies, competing internal and external enterprises create a bias towards expanding capacity and adding to reserves – subject to commercial and political risks which are discussed in Chapter 4.

OPEC outside the Middle East

The six OPEC countries outside the Middle East and the CIS – Algeria, Gabon, Indonesia, Libya, Nigeria and Venezuela – contain about 10% of estimated total possible remaining world reserves of conventional[19] oil and supplied about a third of 1994 OPEC production (10% of world production). Their 'identified' R/P ratios lie closer to those of the 'Rest of World' than those of the Middle East. Indonesia (R/P 25) has maintained a strong private-sector participation. Nigeria (R/P 26-29),[20] with continuing private-sector participation, has improved its terms. Algeria (oil R/P 20) has opened the onshore fields (mainly gas) to the private sector in the 1990s. Venezuela (R/P 54-65)[21] has taken steps down the competitive road in offering opportunities for participation in light oil development ('field rehabilitation contracts' in 1994), offering significant discovered fields and exploration acreage for bidding in 1995, and at the time securing 'strategic alliances' for the conversion of non-conventional crude oil.

The diffusion of private-sector technology could increase production potential in these areas in the same way as it has in the 'Rest of World', though the initial thrust is on cost reduction. Moreover, private-sector com-

---

[19] 'Conventional' as defined in the Masters paper. The assumption about the recovery rates of the large reserves of varying degrees of heavy oil (10–20 degree API) in Venezuela gives this estimate a margin of error.
[20] Using Masters' reserve figures. On the lower proved reserve figures reported in the *BP Statistical Review* the ratio is 11. There are smaller differences for the same reason in the other ratios quoted.
[21] Difference between two sources for reserves, possibly connected with the definition of conventional oil or the estimate of economically recoverable heavy conventional oil: R/P ratios for oil below 17 degrees API are much higher.

petitive development and exploration could also expand the reserve base. These countries have shown little evidence, since 1989, of seriously restraining for policy or 'cartel' reasons the growth of their production potential or indeed of their production: Venezuela is currently producing significantly above its OPEC quota.

Middle East, non-OPEC

A small group (about 1% of world reserves and 1% of world production) of minor Middle Eastern producers are outside OPEC but for most of the purposes of this book are treated with the Middle East. Their R/P ratios are relatively low (16 for Oman, 12 for Syria, 33 for Yemen – but Yemen production is currently being expanded.) These non-OPEC countries, like the OPEC countries outside the Middle East, have maintained opportunities for international private-sector participation and most have tended to make the terms for that participation more attractive since 1986.

The Middle East OPEC countries

The size of the oil reserves in Middle East OPEC countries is, in aggregate, very large. There are important differences between them which are discussed in Chapter 3. The policies these countries follow in developing their identified reserves will have, as they have always had, a profound influence on the world oil market, but for the next few decades the size of the identified or future reserve base is likely to be less important than other factors.

The Middle East (including the non-OPEC members discussed above) contains 54% of the world's remaining 'identified',[22] and 25% of 'undiscovered' estimated reserves, giving a total of 45% of likely remaining oil reserves and an R/P ratio of 89 for identified reserves and

---

[22] This is a lower figure than the 65% shown in the *BP Statistical Review*, 1995, which reproduces data published in the *Oil and Gas Journal* of 26 December 1994. Masters uses higher figures for reserves for other parts of the world, based on field data published by Petroconsultants; he found 66 bn bbls of Saudi Arabia's published proved oil reserve figure could not be accounted for by field or other sources. The much quoted figure of 'two-thirds of the world's oil reserves are in the Middle East' is based on commercial publications and on the unsupported Middle Eastern published estimates of 'proved reserves' which were revised upwards during the 1980s, concurrently with negotiations about production quotas.

106 for possible total reserves. The potential for expansion of oil production is different between the major Middle East oil producers. The key geopolitical message from these figures is not the possible constraint of depletion but the potential for competition between Middle Eastern producers seeking to preserve or expand their share of the available oil markets. This theme is developed in Chapter 3.

Future demand

Like production, demand will be a function of price (to consumers, after paying consumption taxes), competition from other fuels and the rate of economic growth. Seven forecasts or 'scenarios' made in 1995 are compared in Figure 2.4. The range of forecasts is narrow: 15% between the highest and the lowest. The World Bank figure of 88 mmbd by 2010 is not constrained by assumptions about significant rises in prices. Figure 2.5 illustrates how such demand might be met:

- The key assumption (which differs from the supply assumptions made in the forecasts quoted) is that production in Rest of World continues to grow steadily at the rate which has been maintained for the past 30 years: 600,000 bd per year. (Most forecasts still repeat the ever-disproved assumption that 'Rest of World' supply will decline within the next 5–10 years from the date of forecast.)
- CIS production is assumed to grow after the year 2000 for the reasons explained in Chapter 4.
- Non-Middle-East OPEC is assumed to grow at a modest rate consistent with past trends and current plans and potential in the countries concerned.
- Middle East supply is assumed to be the balancing supply – a phenomenon which, though conventional, deserves discussion (see below).

In this projection, the Middle East share of world oil production remains close to 30% through the next ten years, rising to 31% by 2010.

Figure 2.4 Oil demand forecast in 1995 for 2010

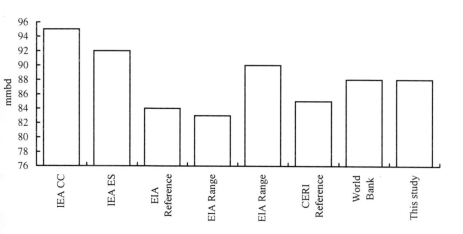

Sources: International Energy Agency (1995e); Energy Information Administration (1995); Canadian Energy Research Institute (1995); World Bank (1995); author.

If the highest demand projection (95 mmbd) is taken, and the difference met entirely from the Middle East, the Middle East share would rise to 36%, its 1975 level. If OPEC producers outside the Middle East are included, the total OPEC percentage share is about 10% higher than for the Middle East.

Implications

Cartelization is a non-problem

The analysis above suggests that the dynamics of oil production and demand, at least until 2010, do not support the idea that the call on OPEC will grow rapidly to unprecedented levels which would make cartelization simple. In fact, the reverse remains true: as long as OPEC R/P ratios remain so much higher than those in the rest of the world, there is no depletion constraint on expanding production by Middle East OPEC members. Each has economic incentives to expand, if (a big if) negative effects on

Figure 2.5 Actual and possible oil production 1965–2010

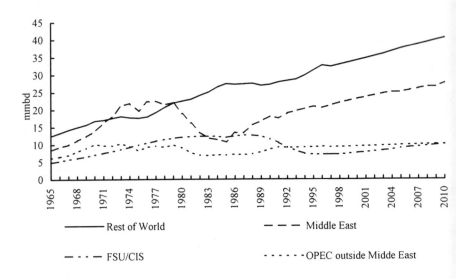

Source: actuals: *BP Statistical Review* (1995); projections: author.

price can be limited. This capacity for expanding production is combined
with the political rivalry described in the next chapter. The argument there
is that the oil producers of the Middle East are driven to compete for market
share by political as well as economic objectives. If competition in the
Middle East is combined with the idea that the Middle Eastern share of
world production is not bound to rise, the outlook for oil prices to 2010 and
perhaps beyond is that oil prices are unlikely to be driven upwards. They
may remain uncertain within a wide band, influenced by short term events,
which may include supply disruptions, and by cyclic movements in capacity
and demand.

The dynamics of oil price formation are complex, and have generally
eluded price forecasters.[23] This study does not aim to rehearse the whole
debate. From the geopolitical point of view, the important cases are at the
extremes: the possibility of 'high' prices – say 50% above present level –
driven by an OPEC or Middle East 'cartel' and the possibility of 'low' prices

---

[23] For a recent review, see Streifel (1995).

Figure 2.6 Oil price forecasts for 2010

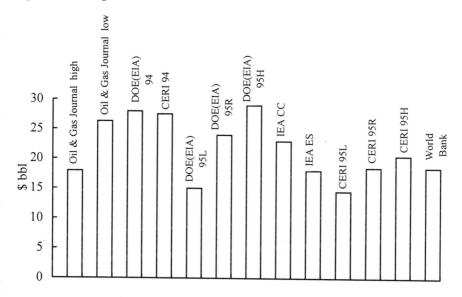

Sources: EIA, IEA, World Bank, CERI.

driven by intense competition between low-cost producers with effects on the political stability of those incapable of continuously expanding production. The first case has mainly been dealt with in this chapter: sustained high prices are unlikely because of the continuing growth of oil supplies outside OPEC and competition within it. The second, 'low' price case is mainly discussed in the next chapter. Between these cases there is scope for cyclical fluctuations, driven by leads and lags in investment in supply and demand, and 'shocks' driven by technical, macroeconomic or political accidents: it is arguable that the last risk is greater, the lower the general level of prices.

Recent oil price forecasts, shown in Figure 2.6, show less variation than these cartoon 'low' and 'high' cases, but conventional wisdom seems to be moving in the direction of flat price forecasts. For planning purposes some companies quote relatively flat prices as their planning assumptions.[24] It might be more accurate to describe these as 'trendless' forecasts, since few would deny the scope for short and medium term volatility.

---

[24] See for example Jennings (1996).

Disruption is the real problem

The other common cause for concern about dependence on the Middle
East oil producers is the risk of disruption of supplies, either because of
deliberate combined political action (as with the Arab oil producers in
1973) or because of domestic or regional political upheavals such as the
Iranian revolution in 1978, or the Gulf war of 1990–1. These risks
undoubtedly exist. The analysis of the next chapter suggests that they are
likely to become more severe, partly because of the failure of oil revenues
to continue rising. Disruptions do not necessarily lead to sustained higher
levels of price.

Policy keynote: the global paradoxes
The production paradox: Middle East versus the rest

The high R/P ratios in the Middle East support the view that Middle East
producers' share of world oil production will increase eventually: the question is when, and what connection will there be with international oil
prices. The signal of high Middle East R/P ratios is ambiguous: it says at
the same time (a) that the high R/P producers in the Middle East may
increase their share of the market, with a supposed risk to consumers of
higher, cartelized prices, but (b) that competition between the same Middle
East producers could dramatically reduce prices until the inventory of
unproduced reserves is brought down towards a more economic ratio. The
ambiguity could be resolved if competitive expansion of capacity in the
Middle East were to drive prices significantly below those at which non-
Middle-East capacity can continue to grow – say below $10 per barrel –
for a sustained period. This period could be quite long: the Middle East as
a bloc has a 95-year inventory, compared to 10 in Europe and the USA.
(Middle East identified oil reserves alone could support current world oil
consumption for almost 30 years.) It would need to be long enough to
choke off expansion of capacity outside the Middle East: variable costs of
production, combined with the high cost of closing down and decommis-
sioning existing facilities, will keep even areas like the North Sea producing through short 3–5-year cycles of 'low' prices.

As the next chapter describes, most Middle East producers will have difficulty in taking the economic strain of today's level of oil prices for the next five years, let alone lower prices for a longer period. Even when the Middle East share of the world oil market grows again, the unequal reserve endowments of the Middle East producers, combined with their political and economic rivalry, make it extremely unlikely that the forces for competitive capacity expansion will be subdued by skilful cartel management to engineer sustained rises in price. This is hardly a scenario which presents oil consumers with a threat of cartelized restraining competition in the short run by means of quotas or parallel policies that support prices. Meanwhile, Middle East and other OPEC producers are likely to continue to use quotas and other price support measures to moderate the effect on price of recurrent short-term surplus capacity.

An alternative resolution of the paradox for Middle East and other low-cost producers is sometimes proposed: that would be to open their oil reserves, on attractive and credible terms, to long-term equity investment by the companies which are currently investing in expanding capacity elsewhere. This is essentially Venezuelan's current policy for part of its expansion programme and will increase its market share. It is possible that if UN sanctions on Iraq and US sanctions on Iran were fully lifted there might be similar developments in those two countries.

The main problem about the idea of slowing investment outside OPEC by attracting funds out of the rest of the world to OPEC is that the arithmetic does not work. Worldwide upstream investment is currently estimated by the Institut Français du Pétrole at around $85 billion, of which about $10 billion is in OPEC.[25] Even doubling OPEC investment would 'divert' only 14% of investment from the rest of the world. The concept of 'diversion' also assumes that the pool of funds available for upstream investment worldwide is limited to current levels of spending (otherwise economic opportunities outside OPEC would still be taken up). The only effective way in which the Middle East producers could limit the private-

---

[25] Estimates published by the Institut Français du Pétrole, 'Investments in the oil and gas sector' *Panorama 96*, IFP Paris, 1996. Estimating expenditure upstream is difficult, since most Middle East oil producers do not publish financial reports on their petroleum industries. These estimates are similar to others published by Chase Bank and the author.

sector funds available for upstream investment elsewhere would be for them to compete so intensely that the oil price falls for a long period. This alternative becomes merely a variation of the first possibility of long-run intense competition for expanding markets: neither threatens oil consumers with aggressively rising, cartelized prices.

Updating public policy

These paradoxical signals generate contradictory responses: the private-sector oil producers prepare for low oil prices by continuing to reduce cost and invest very conservatively while governments of oil-importing countries are still toying with policies opposed to 'oil dependence'. These are supposed to protect their consumers against the risk of cartelized prices, but would, if they were effective, meanwhile deny them the benefits of competition from oil against the non-oil alternatives.

Under the new geopolitics a more rational policy approach for governments of oil-importing countries would be to encourage the process of 'opening' and privatization which makes new oil provinces available for exploration and allows competitive forces to maintain the impetus of development and expansion of discovered reserves anywhere in the world where these reserves are open to international markets. Such an 'extrovert' policy is in practice not so very different from current reality in US and Japanese policies.

In practice, the USA has abandoned the failed objectives of the 1970s of 'energy independence'. Its special incentives for domestic oil and gas production are limited to royalty remission for offshore developments and minor tax reliefs. The US administration gives active political support to the efforts of US companies to explore and develop foreign oil reserves in countries which are not embargoed for political reasons.

The Japanese government has for decades promoted Japanese investment in foreign exploration through the Japanese National Oil Corporation, such that 10% of Japan's oil supplies comes from projects in which Japanese companies participate.

From Europe, the main initiative has been the European Energy Charter, signed in 1991 and followed by the Energy Charter Treaty

(1995). The latter has the effect of applying to energy fuels and energy production services the GATT provisions on non-discrimination for access and transit; committing the signatory countries to provide national treatment for wide classes of energy investment GATT provisions on non-discrimination; and establishing a procedure for binding arbitration to which private foreign enterprises would have direct access. Though most countries in Europe and the former Soviet Union have signed the treaty, most other actual or potential oil producers did not, and the USA, after being active in the negotiations has so far delayed signing. Even in the EU's 1995 White Paper [26] which relaxed many of the anti-oil features of the previous EU energy policy, no policy has been proposed to give political support at European level to the role of international worldwide exploration and production activity in increasing energy supplies and security.

---

[26] European Commission (1995).

Map 3.1: Middle East

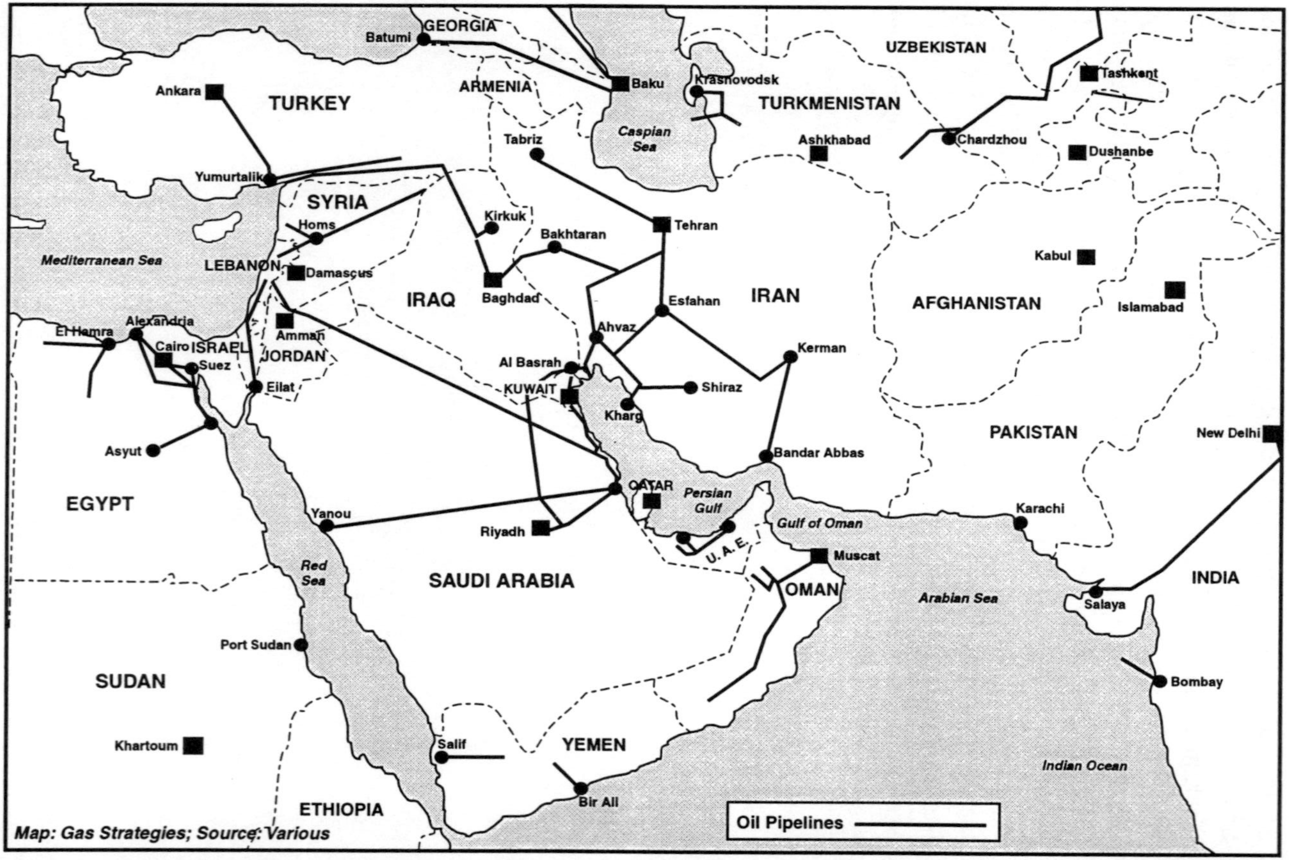

Map: Gas Strategies; Source: Various

Chapter 3

The Middle East

Introduction

This chapter describes three key features of the future petroleum situation in the Middle East:

- the drive to develop a 100-year overhang of reserves;
- the potential for competition driven by the increasing differences, and therefore tensions, between the different producing countries, both in their petroleum potential and in their economic imperatives;
- the tension between a 'cartel' model of supply management – OPEC – and the dominant position of Saudi Arabia while production outside the Middle East continues to increase;.

The short message of this analysis for oil imports and for suppliers of alternative fuels is that the forces driving long-term expansion and competition in the supply of Middle East oil are very strong, but the risks of temporary disruptions are probably increasing.

The capacity to expand capacity
Oil

The previous chapter showed that the Middle East share of the world's oil production may remain at around 30% to the year 2010. The Middle East contains around 45% of all the oil reserves so far identified and estimated to await discovery. The ratio of these reserves to production is an indicator of potential future production in the longer term – the first half of the twenty-first century.

Figure 3.1 Oil production and reserves

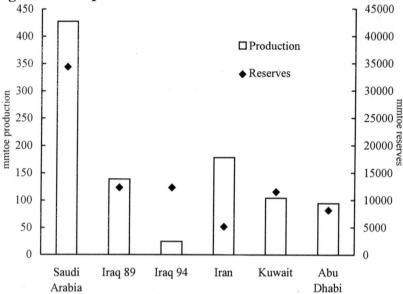

Sources: *BP Statistical Review* (1995), Masters (1994).

Figure 3.1 compares 1994 production (and 1989 production in the case of Iraq) on the left-hand scale with identified[1] reserves of oil on the right-hand scale, which is greater by a factor of 100. Where the reserves tag sits at the top of the production column on the figure, the R/P ratio is 100; where it is below, it is lower. As the figure shows, Iran is the striking exception (apart from Iraq under current sanctions). With an R/P ratio of just under 30,[2] Iran's long-term oil production potential is limited. Exports of oil are further limited because one-third of Iranian oil production is consumed in Iran and the proportion is rising.[3] Iran's long-term future as a petroleum

---

[1] The figures for 'identified' reserves in Masters (1994) are used in preference to other sources because Masters is the only source that publishes estimates of undiscovered reserves. Although there is a wide range of uncertainty on these estimates, they do provide a necessary indicator of differences in future potential which are certainly in the minds of decision-makers.

[2] Since the Masters estimates were compiled, the Iranian government has announced two discoveries with estimated reserves totalling 10 bn bbls (1,360 mtoe). This would increase the R/P ratio by just over 1 year.

[3] The decline in oil exports may be slowed by slowing the growth of domestic oil consumption by raising domestic prices towards export levels.

exporter depends on developing its reserves of natural gas (see below).

Capacity in the medium term to 2000 is the subject of development plans, investment, markets and policy; of these the most important is policy. In Iran plans for higher oil production levels depend on the development of a massive scheme for the gathering and re-injection of gas, mainly from gas fields not associated with oil production.[4] Foreign finance and technology is being sought for this scheme, partly on a contractor basis and partly on a near-equity basis (for offshore fields such as North and South Pars). Foreign interest is limited by US sanctions, and by the commercial terms offered by Iran.

In Abu Dhabi cost is a constraint: projects for heavy oil in complex reservoirs will be at the back of the international development queue. In Kuwait a major programme of expansion would probably require substantial foreign inputs of technical management on terms which are only just beginning to develop.

The timing of oil developments is not hurried by market prospects. The scenario outlined in Chapter 2 suggests that the demand for Middle East oil may not increase significantly before 2000, and by 2010 may increase by only 7 mmbd.

The announced and reported development plans of the region, as summarized by the IEA,[5] are shown in Figure 3.2, compared with the IEA estimate of reported capacity in 1995 and production in 1995.[6] If these plans were fulfilled, there would be capacity in place by 2000 to meet the demand suggested for 2010. In these numbers, unused oil production capacity in these Middle East countries was about 5.7 mmbd in 1995. Of this 2 mmbd was held under duress in Iraq, 1.8 mmbd was held voluntarily in Saudi Arabia and the balance was held elsewhere, broadly in line with OPEC quotas.

---

4 The re-injection of gas occurring in an oil-producing reservoir is common practice worldwide. What is unusual in Iran, with complex reservoir structures, is that many of the gas and oil reservoirs are separated by significant distances as well as geology.

5 IEA (1995b). A figure of 12 mmbd has been substituted for Saudi Arabia, in line with plans announced in the past.

6 IEA provisional estimate, *Oil Market Report*, 6 February 1996.

Figure 3.2 1995 production and capacity, 2000 capacity

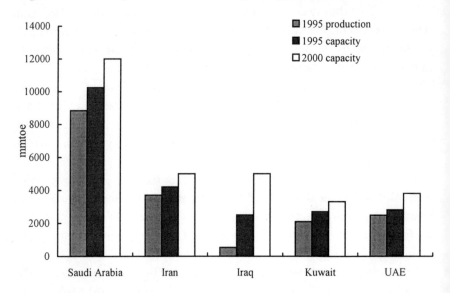

Sources: IEA (1995b).

The reported and announced plans imply an expansion of 4.5 mmbd by the year 2000, of which 2 mmbd will be in Iraq and 1.8 mmbd in Saudi Arabia.[7] In reality, the distribution of expansion might easily be different. It is difficult, writing in 1996, to imagine that Iraq will emerge from sanctions, reach post-sanctions agreements with foreign companies, and double its oil production capacity within four years.

On the other hand, there can be little doubt that Saudi Arabian capacity could be expanded to 12 mmbd, and possibly beyond, even by the year 2000: Saudi Aramco has recently completed a rapid expansion of similar magnitude. A variety of fields has been evaluated for development or expansion. Plans exist for options greater than 12 mmbd. The cost of development in Saudi Arabia is probably the cheapest in the Middle East (except for the rehabilitation of shut-in Iraqi capacity).

---

[7]   On the author's assumptions of 12 mmbd capacity in Saudi Arabia, compared to IEA assumptions of 11.1 mmbd.

Economics are also material to the reality of these expansion plans. To restore pre-war Iraqi capacity would be 'relatively' cheap and the paybacks would be rapid. Initial finance would be required and early oil revenue will be needed to meet all the claims which are likely to form part of any international settlement with Iraq, as well as to provide improvements in the conditions of the Iraqi people. Kuwait and the UAE can undoubtedly fund their expansion. For Saudi Arabia, financing a further $4 bn to expand capacity to 12 mmbd is entirely feasible. The question would be whether the additional capacity would be used when the country already has nearly 2 mmbd of unused capacity and demand is unlikely to increase in the near term. If the alternative is to see capacity expansion, and eventual production increases elsewhere, the economics could stand up. Roughly speaking, an increase in total Saudi production of 250,000 bbls/d would pay off the cost of an incremental 2 mmbd capacity in about three years: the threat would pay its way.

In short, additional capacity will be required, but probably post-2000. Saudi Arabia is best placed to provide its current share, or more, at relatively short notice, while expansion in Iraq and Iran will be delayed by the sanctions against those countries, and by the (not unrelated) need to engage substantial foreign technical and financial resources which are not at present accessible on mutually satisfactory terms.

Gas

For gas, the situation is different. As Figure 3.3 shows, most producers have R/P ratios far in excess of 100 years – in the case of Iran nearly 1,500. Production has been limited to domestic use – which includes gas for re-injection into oil reservoirs to maintain pressure and therefore oil production. It also includes (in Saudi Arabia and Abu Dhabi) gas feedstocks for petrochemicals and for metal smelters. Only Abu Dhabi produced gas for export in 1994 (as 3.8 mtoe LNG). For practical purposes, therefore, gas reserves in the main Middle East exporters are unlimited. Developments are limited by markets.

Figure 3.3 Gas production and reserves

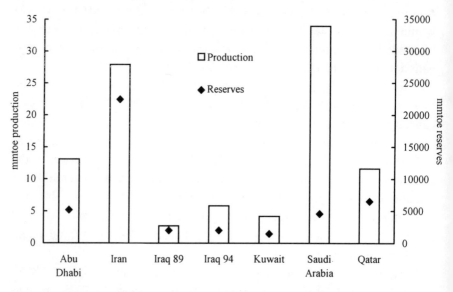

Sources: production: *BP Statistical Review* (1995); reserves: Masters (1994).

In Iran, future gas production is critically important, both to sustain oil production by re-injection and to enhance export revenue which cannot be expanded by significantly higher oil production. The limitations are money, technology and markets. Iran's reserves of gas are in complex structures of varying sizes. The first call on gas production from dry gas fields is for re-injection into oil reservoirs. There is also scope for further substituting gas for oil as fuel for industrial and electricity generation. Reserves would also support export projects. Turkey is one possibility. A pipeline to Russia exists, but the 'switch arrangements' (Iranian gas to Russia, exchanged for Russian gas for Western Europe) had doubtful economic logic when constructed in the 1970s: they have no place in the current Russian gas scene (described in Chapter 4). There is a project concept for a gas pipeline to Pakistan.

All these Iranian projects require large capital investment, foreign technical management (at least in the construction stage), and imports of foreign equipment. The current political relationship between Iran and the

USA prevents US companies – a major part of the international contracting and developing industry – from taking part, and the general economic and political relationships between Iran and the rest of the world are not attractive to large investments of foreign capital in long-term projects requiring stable relationships between exporter and importers who will be dependent on dedicated supplies of gas through LNG or pipeline schemes.

In Abu Dhabi, LNG export capacity was expanded from 2.5 mt to 4.3 mt per year from 1995. Abu Dhabi gas is mostly associated with oil production, and oil and gas capacity expansion will remain broadly linked. Foreign equity-type participation, as well as long-term contracts for gas exports, are characteristic of the Abu Dhabi petroleum industry.

The Qatar gas dome is one of the largest single gas accumulations in the world: unit costs of production will be low. After long and difficult negotiation Qatar has concluded agreements with foreign partners and customers for a 6 mta LNG export project, to begin production in 1997. A further 10 mth (the two Rasgas projects) are the subject of letters of intent. There have been conceptual schemes for 15 mta LNG beyond that – probably for production post-2010.

This gas would be competing in an East Asian market concerned about diversification of energy supplies – see Chapter 5. There are a number of conceptual projects for pipeline export, mostly involving a combination of sources for export to Pakistan and India. These could be on the policy agenda before 2000.

Geology ahead

In the longer term, some allowance must be made for future discoveries of oil and gas. Even with the wide range of uncertainty that accompanies such estimates, it is possible to see which countries can base their long-term economic development on continuing the expansion of oil production well into the next century, and which must find ways to develop large-scale gas exports to supplement and increasingly replace relatively limited oil exports. Figure 3.4 summarizes the contrasting long-term potential.

This distribution of actual and potential resources has implications for the countries' long-term interests.

Figure 3.4 Petroleum (oil and gas) reserves

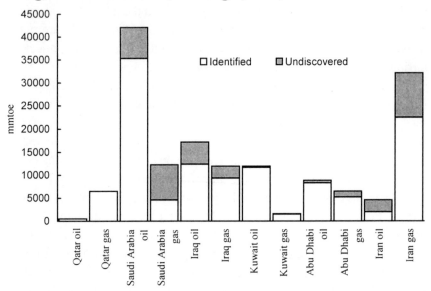

Sources: BP Statistical Review (1995) and Masters (1994).

Saudi Arabia is the most important oil country with 39% of the region's identified oil reserves and probably 45% of the sum of identified plus undiscovered reserves. It also has the capacity, and the demonstrated ability, to expand its production rapidly at relatively short notice. Iraq and Iran do not have that capacity.

Even when allowance is made for the ultimate development of Iran's gas reserves, Saudi Arabia will be the most important petroleum country – with about 35% of the combined oil and gas reserves of the total petroleum reserves of the region.

Iran is in the critical position of needing foreign inputs to develop its gas potential.

The mixture of oil and gas potential differs between countries: oil is what is being produced today; gas is a future long-term option which is critical for Iran as well as the much smaller Qatar, and valuable for Abu Dhabi.

The current production and the expansion of future potential are seriously distorted by the sanctions on Iraq. The longer term balance between the producing countries will change.

Managing competition

Managing capacity expansion is a new experience for the governments of many oil exporting countries. Before 'participation' and nationalization of the private sector in most of these countries in the late 1970s, expansion plans depended on investment by a relatively small number of international private-sector oil companies, whose interests and access to resources were geographically diverse and flexible. National interests were irrelevant except in so far as they were forced on the companies as conditions of their concessions and property or operating rights.

The capacity planning role for the international private-sector companies disappeared in the major oil exporting countries in the Middle East, and in Venezuela, during the late 1970s. The oil price shock of 1979–80 shifted the private-sector interest in capacity expansion to those countries where it still had a role: capacity expansion in the main oil exporting countries was not an issue because their pricing policies, together with the economic recession and demand response to the oil price shocks, left them holding the worldwide structural surplus of capacity which was still present in 1995.[8]

As the need for new capacity grows nearer, the expectations in the short-term market are influenced by the evidence of potential for expanding capacity and plans to carry out the kind of expansion (described above).

---

[8] The question of future capacity expansion was discussed in OPEC in the late 1970s as part of the 'Long Term Strategy'.

Figure 3.5 1994 petroleum (oil and gas) production

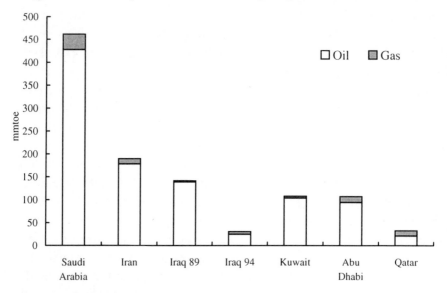

Source: *BP Statistical Review* (1995).

Managing spare capacity: failing at an old game

The competition that matters in the near term in the Middle East is competition for the oil market that remains when all other producers have produced and sold what they can. Gas is not a factor, except for Iran and Qatar, whose gas expansion schemes compete with Russian, Norwegian and Algerian gas in European markets and with Russian and Pacific gas in Asian markets. Figure 3.5 shows the relative importance of oil and gas production in 1994. With Iraq's prewar capacity taken into account, the utilization rate of capacity in the Middle East in 1995 was about 75% – the same as in 1989. Expansion (half of it in Saudi Arabia) has matched the 4 mmbd increase in demand over the past five years.[9]

---

[9] These figures accept the Iranian statement that 1995 production capacity is 4.5 mmbd, accounting for nearly a third of the total increase: it is possible that effective capacity utilization in 1995 was higher than 75% for the Middle East as a whole.

For the past 15 years – and probably for the next five – the principal competitive problem for the Middle East producers has been and will be the management of spare capacity to prevent a collapse of the oil price. There is a belief that free-for-all competition has the potential to reduce oil prices dramatically (for some period) to the variable cost of current non-OPEC production and in the longer term to the cost of development of new non-Middle-East supplies on a supply curve which probably runs from $5 to $10 per barrel on a full-cost, long-run basis.[10]

Meanwhile, there is an underlying struggle between the producers for oil revenue. No producer wants multilateral disarmament of the oil 'wealth-weapon'. This story shows a tension between two alternative models of supply management, which can be characterized as the 'OPEC cartel' and the 'market leader'.

The cartel model

For the cartel model to work easily, certain conditions are helpful. For OPEC they have progressively weakened over the past 15 years and are likely to weaken further.

- *A known and stable level of underlying capacity.* In OPEC capacities have been changed, even over the past 15 years, as a result of investment by some countries (Saudi Arabia in particular) and disasters in some countries (Iran and Iraq in particular). As was shown in the previous section, production capacities in 1996 are out of line with potential

---

[10] Broadly speaking, a range around $10 would sustain continuing production from more prolific non-OPEC suppliers such as the North Sea and the USA but this supply would – as has long been predicted for other reasons – gradually decline if it were perceived that these prices would last for 10–20 years so that investments in new field developments could not be justified. The weight of demand would then shift rapidly to the low-cost suppliers, who under free-for-all competition could profitably raise their production capacity, if there were no depletion or policy intervention, at supply prices in the range $5–10. Probably only one country – Saudi Arabia – could expand capacity and production rapidly enough, to survive such conditions economically for more than a year or two. Whether it could survive under those conditions politically in a region dependent on current prices for oil revenues is a moot question.

future production capacity as indicated by oil reserves. Further changes in relative capacities in the next 15 years are inevitable.

- *A reasonably good understanding of the demand for the commodity.* Since 1979, however, producers and consumers of oil alike have been surprised by unexpected elasticities in the demand for fuels in response to price, and by increased competition from other fuels – notably gas for power generation through combined cycle turbine plants.
- *A high share of the market.* Oil's share of the total energy market is not likely to grow.[11] The Middle East share of world oil production, at its highest at 37% in 1973, has now declined to 30% and may remain there until 2010 and possibly beyond. The result is that any production control mechanism faces a gearing effect: to achieve a 5% reduction in world oil supply the Middle East's must reduce supply by 15%. It is of course in the interests of the 'cartel core' to share any production restraint as widely as possible. The OPEC share has followed a similar path at about 10% above the Middle East level. However, since 1991 Venezuela, the major producer outside the Middle East with large long-term reserves, has appeared to abandon restraint and not only to produce what the market for its particular suite of crudes will bear but to expand crude production capacity.
- *A stable and relatively inflexible market mechanism.* This was provided in OPEC's early years by negotiations with the companies; then, during the 1970s, by participation and buy-back agreements. The development of formal commodity markets, futures markets and over-the-counter trading in all principal consuming areas has dramatically opened the trading system, exposing the relatively small number of crude producers to the demands of very large numbers of competing refining companies and even end users able to hedge the crude element in their product purchasing exposures.
- *The cartel must have some effective sanction against producers who do not cooperate.* As price expectations have lowered over the past ten years, the effective sanctions become more cataclysmic. A period of

---

[11]   See IEA (1995e). The share of oil is stable to 2010 in the 'capacity constrained' case and falls in the 'energy-saving' case.

'free-for all' would repeat the degree of competition of 1985–6, starting from a lower price base.

With hindsight, it may be that the classic 'cycle of fear and greed' in OPEC is over.[12] It began with the decision of 16 October 1973 to announce unilateral price increases, following the breakdown of negotiations with the international companies. A complex period followed during which OPEC attempted to achieve implicit revenue objectives by setting marker and differential price targets. This broke down during the second oil shocks and led to the decision of 26–27 March 1979, which allowed countries unilaterally to add premiums to their 'official' prices. By 1981, with prices on their way down, OPEC marker prices reappeared in conjunction with production ceilings and quotas which did not apply to Saudi Arabia.[13] Saudi Arabia's position as a 'swing producer' eventually became intolerable because of the loss of output and revenue.

In 1985, through the introduction of 'netback pricing', Saudi Arabia began to act to recapture market share – and incidentally destroyed the last vestiges of the long-term contract pricing system. Spot prices fell at times below $10 until, in autumn 1986, all OPEC members agreed on a set of quotas which genuinely restricted output and did not require Saudi Arabia to absorb future shortfalls in demand or increases in supply by others. Quotas, with a loosely expressed price target, replaced prices as the controls for sharing out the available market.

Management by quota may be said to have ended in November 1994 when, with Iraq exports embargoed by the UN, quotas were not adjusted to either price or demand targets but 'rolled over'. This move cleverly removed from the OPEC ministers the responsibility for 'micromanaging' supply on a quarterly basis and cut away the speculative fever – generally adverse to the exporters – which tended to accompany OPEC ministerial meetings.

---

[12] For a classic analysis of this period, see Adelman (1995) and Hartshorn (1994). There is also a short sketch in Mitchell (1994) which attempts to explain how the price increases of 1973 and 1978–9 were initially sustained by factors not collectively managed by the oil exporters.

[13] From 1983.

Figure 3.6 1995 production versus past peaks

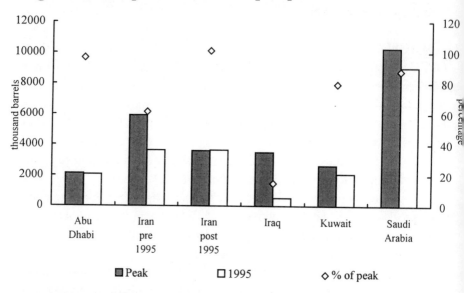

Source: *BP Statistical Review* (1995).

In some respects, the OPEC Ministers' decision to move away from an operational price-setting role was analogous to the UK government's decision, over ten years earlier, to remove the British National Oil Corporation from its central role in trading North Sea oil. (This had led to the British government being blamed for everything that was considered to be wrong with the world oil price.) In effect, OPEC Ministers said in 1994: 'You know what we will produce: if the price falls because other producers continue to expand production and show no restraint, it is their responsibility, not ours.'

But if OPEC governments do not attempt to balance demand and supply on a short-term basis, what is their role? By the end of 1995 Venezuela was producing almost 500,000 bd above its OPEC quota. Nigeria and Algeria held minimal spare capacity as a result of their quotas. As Figure 3.6 shows, within the Middle Eastern core of OPEC in 1996 half of almost 5 mmbd of spare capacity is allocated to Iraq by UN sanction. Except in Iraq, production in 1995 was over 80% of previous peak production. For post-revolutionary Iran and for Abu Dhabi it was almost 100% of past peaks. The full return of Iraq to the market any time before the end of the century will be the final test of the 'cartel' model.

The end of the 'cartel' model for managing Middle East supplies in the future would not mean the 'end of OPEC'. The organization provides a forum in which the oil ministers of the principal Middle East exporting countries can meet to discuss essential oil matters on a multilateral basis. Signalling and negotiation will always form part of the relationships between the Middle East exporters, and facilitating these activities will always be a useful role, even when the main decisions are taken outside the OPEC ministerial meetings.[14]

The 'dominant producer' model

Saudi Arabia has for twenty years played a role which has been partly expressed through its bargaining position in securing OPEC decisions – and therefore collaboration by other producers – and partly through its independent actions. Saudi Arabia acted independently on several important occasions. In the late 1970s it maintained long-term contract prices to Aramco partners which gave them, supposedly, an advantage of oil priced on shorter-term markets. In 1985, Saudi Arabia introduced 'netback' pricing, also on long-running contractual relationships, to protect its exports and signal its intention to regain market share. Saudi reluctance to accept a nominal quota reflects its real production power as well as a constitutional reluctance to admit any element of international control over its oil production policy.

Through price expectations the challenge of managing supply from the Middle East is changing from the task of managing spare capacity to the task of management of capacity expansion. In the task of managing surplus capacity Saudi Arabia has a strong position because:

---

[14] This would not be new: in 1973 the Shah effectively scooped OPEC by first announcing unilateral price increases. In 1970, Libya had pre-empted OPEC in agreeing posted prices.

- it is a large producer.
- until the Gulf war, it had substantial external financial reserves and could withstand periods of low revenue, whether caused by low prices or low volumes.
- the variable costs of production are low. Saudi Arabia exemplifies the unique feature about the economics of oil: it tends to generate large rents which accrue to the government of the producing country without involving the rest of the economy.[15] In economists' terms, the cost of changing the level of production in the short term is almost entirely opportunity cost: workers do not need to be laid off or hired (in Saudi Arabia a high proportion of those engaged in the oil industry and the related technical support services are expatriates anyway).
- finally, Saudi Arabia has had at all times an endowment of spare capacity as a result of past investment, and this is likely to continue. As a result, in the short term it has the flexibility to vary production upwards (as it did in 1979 and 1990–1) as well as downwards. This gives it the critical ability to sustain total revenues in the event of a price war.

Given these factors, competing producers will be influenced more and more by Saudi Arabian policy. In the short term it has more options than they do. In the long term Saudi Arabia can enlarge those options because of its reserve base, the advanced state of knowledge about the potential, its planning for development projects, the proven organizational ability to carry out such projects (using foreign inputs where necessary on terms which are established and well understood), the relatively low cost of increasing capacity and the speed with which projects can be developed. The competitors in the Middle East, such as Kuwait and Abu Dhabi, which might have the financial resources to engage in an investment race with Saudi Arabia, do not have the oil reserves to do so on a large scale, and would also require foreign inputs to execute ambitious expansion plans.

---

[15] As Professor Halliday points out (Halliday 1996), 'The uniqueness of oil resides . . . in the peculiar form of payment resulting from it, rent to producer states that does not entail the forward and backward linkages with the rest of the economy that are characteristic of primary production in the Third World. The collection of this "rent" enables the producer state, and those controlling it, to amass enormous sums of money without engaging in any form of production; it is this which has generated such major social tensions within the producer states.'

Figure 3.7 Middle East oil production shares

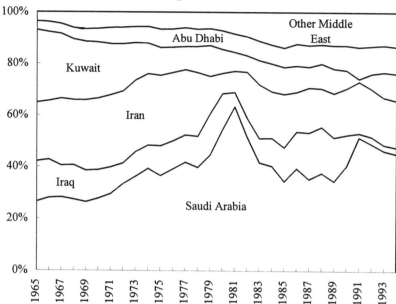

Source: BP Statistical Review (1995).

The others are less well placed. Iraq, which has large identified oil reserves for development, would require foreign funds and probably also technical input. Many sources of these are denied as a result of UN sanctions. Even if these were lifted, appropriate terms have to be negotiated and a pattern of confidence and trust established with the foreign companies to an extent for which there is no precedent in Iraq's recent history (the last decade of the concessions, before 1971, was marked by low investment and bitter disputes between the government and the foreign companies).

In Iran foreign input of finance and technical management are certainly needed to carry out a major expansion of gas production and the related re-injection programme without which oil production will decline rather than increase. There has been a more recent history of working relationships with foreign contractors (but not with equity investors), but not in major new oil development projects. US companies, and perhaps other foreign companies, are inhibited by US sanctions. The general conditions for foreign investment are difficult.

Figure 3.8 Population and petroleum

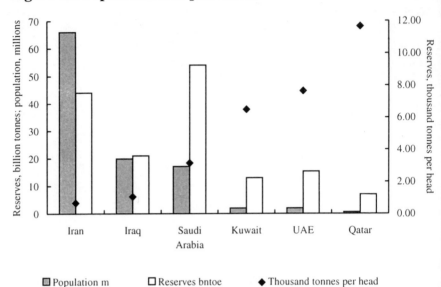

☐ Population m   ☐ Reserves bntoe   ◆ Thousand tonnes per head

Sources: IEA (1995b), Masters (1994), *World Development Report 1995*.

In short, it seems likely that for the next five and probably more years Saudi Arabia will be able to manage competition to expand capacity by the simple exercise of its dominant position. In the shorter term this will influence expectations and reinforce its bargaining position with the other producers. This would be no more than a continuation of the trend which has developed over the past thirty years, and which has fundamentally changed the potential role of OPEC – and of the 'cartel model' in Middle East competition for oil markets. Figure 3.7 illustrates this. In 1965 Kuwait, Iran and Saudi Arabia produced comparable shares of the Middle East oil supply; in 1994 Saudi Arabia supplied 45%. The losers have been the three principal producing rivals: in the case of Iraq for political reasons; in the case of Iran for a combination of political reasons (pre-revolutionary capacity and development plans were never restored) and resource constraints. In the case of Kuwait the conservative production policy introduced in the 1970s became embedded in the OPEC quotas of the 1980s.

Macroeconomics of oil producers

Population

Population structure and trends are part of the Middle East competitive equation. The 1995 World Bank Development Report puts Kuwait and the UAE – with populations of around 2 million each and with GDP in 1993 of $22 bn and $35 bn respectively – in the GDP per capital league table with western Europe and Singapore. Saudi Arabia is reported to have a population of 17 million, Iran 64 million, and Iraq about 20 million. Some of these estimates, which include immigrant workers and refugees, might be regarded as high. The relationships between population and reserves of oil and gas combined varies, as Figure 3.8 shows. Two-thirds of Iran's reserves are gas, unlikely to be developed in the near term, so that in terms of active petroleum wealth, Iran is more comparable to Iraq than to Saudi Arabia.

Population growth in the Middle East oil exporting countries is among the most rapid in the world, supplemented by immigration (or emigration in the case of Kuwait since 1990). In Saudi Arabia, GDP has matched population growth, with the catch-up occurring since 1991. In Kuwait, the population has been drastically reduced by preventing the re-entry of much of the migrant worker population, and by the expulsion of long-term Palestinian migrants, after the Gulf war.

Because of their dependence on petroleum, GDP in all Middle East oil producers fell dramatically in the mid-1980s – by an average of around 5% per annum. In Iran, and in Iraq even before the Gulf war, population growth has run ahead of GDP growth, as Table 3.1 shows.

Economic data for the Middle East oil exporting countries, in the rare cases where such information made public, tend to be incomplete. Everywhere petroleum is the major source of export revenue (see Table 3.2). The data are generally for 1993. In the UAE most of the balance is provided by the export of energy-ntensive products such as alumina. Petroleum is also the major direct source of government revenue – a large part of the balance in the cases of Saudi Arabia and Kuwait being investment income from foreign assets. The capacity of all these economies to invest surpluses abroad in the early 1980s practically disappeared when oil prices fell.

Table 3.1 GDP and population change, 1985–93

	Real GDP (%)*	Population (%)
Iran	+15	+34
Iraq	-77**	+25
Saudi Arabia	+38	+35
Kuwait	+28	-17
UAE	+12	+33
Qatar	+17	+56

*In constant local currency.
**-23% to 1989.
Source: IEA (1995b).

Table 3.2 Importance of oil revenues

	Oil as % of exports	Oil as % of government revenue
Iran	97	64
Iraq	97	n.a.
Saudi Arabia	87	76
Kuwait	95	84
UAE	56	n.a.
Qatar	77	90

Source: IEA (1995b).

Table 3.3 External sector of oil-exporting economies

	Foreign assets $ bn	Foreign debt $ bn	Current account $ bn
Iran	6	16	1
Iraq	5	23	0
Saudi Arabia	56	19	-14
Kuwait	4	10	1
UAE	7	11	0
Qatar	1	2	0

Source: IEA (1995b).

Only Saudi Arabia retains a substantial portfolio of foreign assets. The quality of this is uncertain: it includes claims against government debtors in the region including Iraq. Moreover, during 1993–4 internal government deficits were financed by local borrowing through the banks, in turn financed by the repatriation of private foreign assets attracted by high local rates of interest: the true net position is thus probably less favourable than the (mainly 1993) data in Table 3.3 show. Since 1993 the Saudi current account balance improved in 1994 to a negative of $9 bn – implying there is still an inflow of finance from abroad. With increasing oil production Kuwait achieved a current account surplus of $3 bn in 1994. Both trends probably continued in 1995.

All countries are 'high absorbers' now. The accumulation of foreign surpluses undoubtedly provided time for the exporting countries to begin the necessary process of adjustment to lower oil revenues. The Gulf war brought that adjustment time to an end as the surpluses were run down to pay for the war. The years 1993–5 saw the difficult beginnings in Iran and Saudi Arabia of a process of tightening control on government spending, seeking new sources of revenue by raising prices for goods and services from very low subsidized levels, and cutting back government expenditure, including expenditure by state enterprises.

These efforts probably mean that Saudi Arabia will achieve its projected budget balance for 1996–7, after depending in recent years on a rapid expansion of internal debt. Saudi Arabia probably still has room for manoeuvre within its spending budget, about a third of which is for military and security purposes – much of it for the import of high-tech weaponry and aircraft. This business may well be more important to the arms and aircraft exporting countries (principally the USA and the UK) than to the immediate needs of Saudi defence: orders can be postponed, 'stretched' or even cancelled. Saudi Arabia would also be a good economic candidate for external borrowing: it has relatively low ratios of external debt to GDP (around 15%) and of debt service to exports (around 4%).

Iran, after a period of rapidly escalating very short-term indebtedness, appears to have achieved a degree of internal budget stability, and external stability is forced upon it by the difficulty of raising new debts or credits. Changes in the Majlis and the presidency may need to occur before further steps are politically feasible. New net external borrowing is unlikely. Some rescheduling of existing debts needs to come first. Iran is in theory planning to finance with the help of foreign contractors and equity-type investors the gas developments it needs so badly. This process has yet to get under way and is constrained by US sanctions.

In Kuwait, the mismatch between expectations and revenue resources has been partly avoided by dramatic reductions in the population – even if little government revenue reached the migrant workforce directly, they benefited from subsidized prices and from the spending habits of their employers. In Kuwait, the UAE and Qatar the absolute level of GDP per capita is the highest in the Gulf and austerity will continue to be a relative term – which does not mean that it will be politically insignificant.

The prospect for the near and medium term holds no relief: oil prices are unlikely to increase even in nominal terms while capacity in the Middle East is expanding faster than the call upon it for five years and beyond, and the only substantial increase in volume that can be expected will be for Iraq when sanctions are lifted. That will need to be matched by reductions in volume elsewhere.

Precisely because the greater part of the oil revenue flows through the government budget rather than through private business and labour, the governments are directly responsible for what will be a continuously tightening process of restraining spending (from which individuals benefit) and seeking to raise money without (in the Gulf countries) introducing corporation, personal or consumption tax bases. This is the political curse of the *rentier* economy.

In the Gulf countries the barriers at the summit of power are personal – the ruling families. Mobilizing their people to accept a steady restriction in the flow of benefits will be a political challenge which Europe has not seen since the time of Colbert. How far the mobilization of consent will lead these countries along the democratic road remains to be seen: only in Kuwait is an elected assembly in place.

The political outlook

The policies of the principal Middle East oil producers are driven by three purely political factors which affect their economic and petroleum policies: internal political dynamics, relations with other countries, and rivalry with each other.

Internal political dynamics

The internal political structures specific to each country's religious commitments, constitution and culture must take the strain of allocating relatively unchanged flows of rents among populations whose numbers are increasing, whose habits have been formed in more prosperous times, and whose expectations are being raised by education. They must also take the strain of increasing communication between the people of these countries and a wider world in which human rights in general, and women's rights in particular, occupy a very different place in the political and judicial processes.

The main Middle East oil producers differ in other respects, and these differences give an edge to other rivalries.

Saudi Arabia is a kingdom based on a compromise between the interests of the Wahabi branch of Islam (from which the monarchy derives its legitimacy as guardian of the Holy Places of Islam) and the ruling family. The compromise is challenged by tensions between Wahabi values and practices and the modernizing trends which have accompanied the consumption of the oil wealth by its citizens, especially the principal families. The education of women in particular contrasts with their exclusion from many social activities. Political flexibility derives from the ability of the House of Saud to produce an undisputed succession of wise and capable monarchs, and possibly to a small degree on further progress on the consultative institution surrounding the nominated and private Majlis-al Shura.

Iran is an Islamic republic in which there is an active elected parliament with some authority (particularly over economic matters), considerable freedom of expression, and a degree of political pluralism. More than any other Middle Eastern country, it can be said to have a political structure with an evident capacity for change and evolution: the political role of the clergy is not absolute, nor is the power of the government.

Among the many questions on which internal consensus is needed is the role of foreign business in the future development of the republic: until this becomes more clear, and more positive, the large-scale gas development programmes described earlier will remain limited to isolated projects.

Iraq is an absolute, terror-driven dictatorship in a country with more secular traditions: whether the traditional balance between the three regions of Iraq can be rebuilt after Saddam's rule ends can only be judged when that rule ends. Iraq could spend a long time in the 'dungeon of history'.[16]

The smaller countries vary from *Kuwait*, with a tradition of parliamentary process and opposition, to the traditional rulerships of *Abu Dhabi, Qatar, Oman* and the smaller Gulf countries. All countries are experiencing internal social, economic and religious stress which is becoming more difficult to manage by established political processes. Succession, and stability in the competence of government, are key issues. Relationships with foreign businesses in the petroleum sector are well established in all these countries (except Kuwait, where they are still evolving).

These differences contribute to regional rivalry: democratization – or at least a movement towards it – in one country will, if successful, encourage similar trends elsewhere. Religious differences, and related rules of social behaviour, may also spill over national boundaries, which do not coincide with Islamic differences.

Relations with other countries

The Middle Eastern oil producers have different relationships with countries outside the region which have economic, religious, political or military power to project within it: for all countries in the region, this means principally the United States.

The USA has formal defence agreements, allowing the pre-positioning of military supplies on national territory and the carrying out of military exercises, with Kuwait, Abu Dhabi and Bahrain. An agreement is under

---

[16] Robert Mabro's phrase when speaking at the Institut Français du Pétrole's 'Panorama' Seminar in Paris, 25 January 1996.

negotiation with Qatar and there are complex relationships with Oman (which also has a history of defence cooperation with, and assistance from, the UK). The US web of relationships with Saudi Arabia, by far the most important, is not embodied in a formal overall mutual security agreement. Nevertheless, the US military continues to be involved with the Saudi forces in training programmes, the operation of high-tech equipment, the provisions of information gained by satellite surveillance, and of course the supply and maintenance of weapons, tanks and aircraft. The UK and France are also involved in supplying aircraft, tanks and weapons throughout the Gulf and have defence agreements with Kuwait.

The US is not a new participant in the security of the area: weapons were supplied to Iraq during the Iran–Iraq war; the USA led an operation to convoy tankers threatened by Iran in international waters and thereby secured the continued export of Iraqi and Kuwaiti crude through the Gulf.

The Gulf war made real the intervention that had previously been merely conjecture. The combination of events was uniquely favourable to US intervention: Saddam Hussein's actions contradicted Arab unity; the end of the Cold War and the domestic distractions in the former Soviet Union meant that the USSR (and later Russia) did not have the resources or perhaps the will to assist Iraq, their former client. Last but not least, the immediacy and decisiveness of the US reaction, both political and military, carried an irresistible logic: intervention was real and it worked in its prescribed objective of protecting Saudi Arabia and restoring the independence of Kuwait from Iraq.

With a less conducive combination of circumstances, future US intervention might be more conjectural. In particular, it is not clear under what circumstance the US might try, or carry off, intervention in a situation in which oil supplies were disrupted by purely domestic events. But there is a precedent, there is operating experience, and US *matériel* is 'prepositioned' in the Gulf.

The US policy of 'dual containment' of Iraq and Iran is the obverse of its relationship with Saudi Arabia and the Gulf states. It has a profound effect on the economies and the petroleum sectors of these countries. Because of UN sanctions, which are consistent with the policy of dual containment, some 2 mmbd of Iraqi production capacity is not producing; US and some other foreign companies are debarred from supplying finance and services to Iraq or making equity investment to develop and expand its oil potential. These sanctions could be brought to an end by Security Council acceptance that Iraq was complying with the relevant UN resolutions. A situation might arise in which the USA could not control the outcome of a Security Council decision.

US sanctions specifically against Iran effectively blockade the supply of finance, services, technology and investment by US companies to Iran, critically necessary for the maintenance of oil production in the medium term and the development of gas production in the longer term. Ending these sanctions is entirely at US discretion. Sympathetic sanctions by other countries might be removed if Iran were seen to their satisfaction to take certain actions which the sanctioning countries seek: the repeal (or effective nullification) of the *fatwa* on Salman Rushdie in the case of the UK, and clear separation from the alleged support of international terrorism in the case of many other countries. The question of nuclear proliferation is also relevant: are treaty commitments enough to satisfy the potential suppliers of nuclear energy technology that such supplies do not enhance the risk of proliferation?

Russia has also some possibilities in the region. Even under present conditions it has some leverage with Iran and Iraq through its ability to supply nuclear technology and conventional arms. Through its oil companies, it also has some possibility of investment to enable these countries (for example in Iraq) to create the means to pay for nuclear technology and weapons supplies. However, the financial pump has to be primed and for the time being none of the parties has the means to prime it.

Finally, though the countries share a common hostility to *Israel*, and are not participants in the Middle East peace process, their engagements have been different. Iraq has fought Israel and recently attacked it with Scud missiles. Iran under the Shah had commercial relations with Israel. The Islamic Republic is alleged to support terrorist groups active in seeking to disrupt the peace process. Saudi Arabia, for long a funder of Palestinian movements, remains at a distance rather than openly subversive of the peace process.

Underlying national rivalry

The final factor is the rivalry of the most populous nations with each other. Iraq, with the largest army, has made war on Iran, Kuwait and Saudi Arabia. All countries have, on occasion, probably supported some dissident groups in the others, and in other countries in the region such as Egypt and the Sudan. Saudi Arabia has or has had border disputes with Abu Dhabi and Yemen, and Iran has disputes over Gulf islands with its southern neighbours.

In each of these three political dimensions the principal Middle East oil producing countries are as different as they are in petroleum endowments and in populations and economic profile. Rivalry between Iran, Iraq and Saudi Arabia therefore has many strands: for influence over the smaller Gulf countries; influence in Arab–Israeli relationships; influence in the Arab world generally; and influence in the international congregation of Islam. These countries compete for external support by way of arms and finance. The wealth that oil can bring is a very important weapon against the others. Their oil policies cannot avoid reflecting this fact.

Non-oil rivalry generates oil competition between the principal Middle East producers. There is continual tension between this rivalry and the cooperation necessary to prevent competition in the short term oil market from driving prices down. As the question of oil competition becomes more and more a question of managing the growth of producing capacity the rivalry will become more imperative.

Conclusions: the geopolitical keynotes

The main conclusion of this analysis, therefore, is that sector, macroeconomic and political forces lead to and mutually reinforce competition between the principal oil producers. In combination with the endowment of oil resources in the Middle East, potential supplies from the Middle East are likely to continue to grow rather faster than the demand for Middle East oil.

There is another conclusion: the dependence of the Middle East countries on increasing oil revenues, and their inability to secure those revenues

in the near and medium term except by increasing volumes, will increase
the shift of relative market power to Saudi Arabia; the other countries will
face increasing internal strains in accommodating the needs of increasing
and aspirant populations with the political and economic resources which
they have.

As tension *within* the Middle East oil producers increases, tension
between them will increase. The US dual containment policy, and the
threat of renewed US intervention, reinforces the division of interest
between Saudi Arabia and the other major producers, but suppresses the
consequences of that tension for the time being. It is difficult to imagine
that this situation can be perpetuated to the year 2010. Oil importers may
be reassured by the idea that competition between producers has such
strong and persistent roots. They need also to worry that its short term
contradictions may disrupt supplies as dramatically as in each of the last
three decades.

Summary: petroleum and economic outlook

- Things will not get easier for the people of the Middle East oil exporting countries in the near to medium term. Their governments have some
options to improve their lot through developments involving export projects with foreign investment, as is taking place in Qatar. In Iraq
improvements must follow the lifting of sanctions, but the timing of that
is quite uncertain. In Iran there are mixed signals from willingness to
consider new projects and continuing political barriers on both sides of
the route to improved international relationships.
- The country best positioned economically is Saudi Arabia. The
increased oil volume since 1990 means that the flow of economic
resources has caught up with population growth. Saudi Arabia also has
external assets and income, the capacity to expand the volume of production, and its dominant position among its Middle East competitors,
giving it many levers to pull in managing the situation.
- So far, all the oil producers in the region are making macroeconomic
adjustments – mainly to their government budgets. The scale of these
adjustments will be large and they need to continue for some years.

The personal responsibility of the ruling families for governing in the Gulf countries suggests that some political consent to the relative austerity that will be required for years to come will be needed from both the ruling families and the rest of the population.

Chapter 4

Russia

Introduction

Since the Second World War, the energy economy of Russia (within the Soviet Union, and with the Comecon countries of Eastern Europe until 1992) was well separated from the rest of the world. Domestic production and consumption were organized through the central planning system. There were, in the early 1980s, increasing exports of oil and gas to Western Europe. The latter, involving pipeline construction through Czechoslovakia to Germany and Italy, was politically controversial between the West European importing countries and the USA, which opposed the building for Cold War reasons. Apart from that, what went on inside the Soviet energy economy was unconnected to Western markets, investment, or energy policy. There was a conceptual wall between the Soviet and related energy arena and 'WOCA' – the world outside the communist area – which was where the data were and where policy debates were possible. This conceptual wall has been destroyed as certainly as the Berlin Wall by the disintegration of the central planning system, the end of Soviet hegemony over Eastern Europe, and finally by the independence of republics such as Ukraine, an important energy consumer, and Azerbaijan, Kazakhstan and Turkmenistan, whose offshore Caspian oil resources could support significant oil and gas exports.

Russia is important in the new geopolitics of energy because of the size of its current production, and even more, the size of its petroleum potential: the rate of development of this potential will affect world supply and demand. Russian policies can affect the development of offshore Caspian oil and gas and the economic progress and even perhaps the viability of those countries.

Russia, together with the countries of the former Soviet Union whose export routes are controlled by Russia, supplied about 25% of Western

Europe's petroleum (oil and gas together) imports from outside Europe in 1994. Over 90% of petroleum consumed in Eastern Europe and Ukraine is supplied by Russia. The continued growth and day-to-day stability of these supplies is of economic and political importance to the ever-enlarging European Union.

The decentralization, privatization and relative liberalization of the Russian economy is connecting its internal petroleum markets to external markets. Russian petroleum enterprises are moving towards integration with the world petroleum industry. Some of these Russian enterprises are very large: Gazprom's hydrocarbon production exceeds that of Saudi Aramco. At the same time, limited opportunities for foreign investment in the Russian petroleum industry are developing. This is becoming integrated into the international system of private-sector trade and investment and the intergovernmental agreements and conventions which provide the framework for that system.

This chapter describes:

- Russian gas production and potential, and politics;
- Russian oil production and potential, and politics;
- Russian interrelations with the 'Near abroad' CIS states;
- the general political context;
- international implications.

Russia – the size of the petroleum potential

For most of the past decade, Russia has produced as much petroleum (oil and gas counted together) as the USA, with the important difference that Russia has been a substantial exporter of both oil and gas while the USA has been a substantial importer of both oil and gas. As Figure 4.1 shows, while US oil production has declined steadily since 1985, Russian oil production has declined very fast since 1988 mainly owing to a collapse of investment. Russian gas production has fallen mainly as the result of a collapse in markets.

The future petroleum prospect for the two countries is very different because of the great difference in their proved and likely undiscovered

Figure 4.1 Russian vs US production

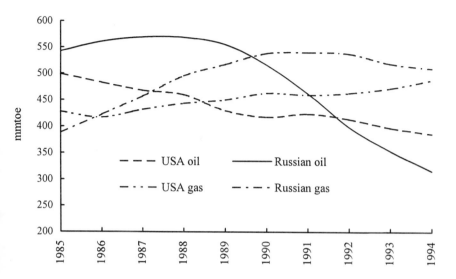

Source: *BP Statistical Review* (1995).

reserves. In future, the US shares of world oil and gas production are likely to fall, while the Russian shares are likely to rise as investment takes place. The ratio of proved reserves to current production in Russia is approximately double that of the USA in the case of oil, and over eight times in the case of gas. Undiscovered reserves also differ in Russia's favour. Though numbers are uncertain for technical and economic reasons, the US Geological Service estimate shows the direction clearly.[1] The USA has 5% of the world's identified petroleum reserves, and Russia, together with Azerbaijan, Kazakhstan and Turkmenistan,[2] has 21%. When the modal estimate (of a wide range for all areas) is added, Russia alone has about 20% of the world total, 25% with the three other CIS countries. It is in the long term half as important as the Middle East and three times as important as the US. Figures 4.2 and 4.3 illustrate these proportions.

---

[1] Masters (1994), updated for 1993 and 1994 production.
[2] Russia is not separated in the Masters numbers. It probably accounts for about 85% of the former Soviet Union – 17% of the world total for identified petroleum reserves and 20% of the identified and undiscovered figure for world petroleum (oil plus gas).

Figures 4.2 Identified reserves

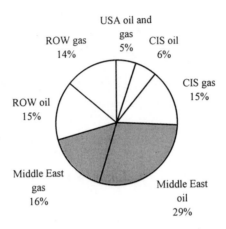

Source: Masters (1994).[3]

Figure 4.3 Identified and undiscovered reserves (modal estimate)

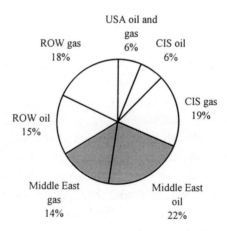

Source: Masters (1994).

---

[3] A comparison between Masters and other estimates of gas reserves is given in the IEA *Natural Gas Security Study* (1995). Masters' figures for identified reserves for Russia are around 25% lower than the others quoted, while his figures for the whole world are within 2% of the other estimates.

Figure 4.4 FSU/Russian gas production

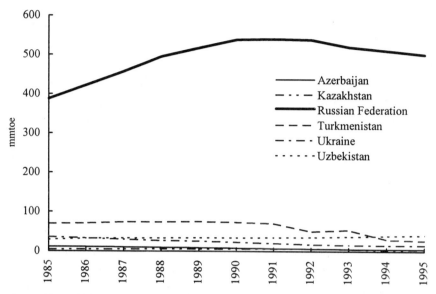

Source: IEA (1995a).

Gas

Gas production

Two-thirds of Russian production comes from two fields – Urengoy, a declining field, and Yamburg, a potentially increasing field. Both are producing below their potential and require additional investment to maintain pressure and to develop small fields near the same infrastructure. Substantial investment is also necessary to maintain and refurbish the transmission system. This is subject to a detailed survey currently being carried out by Gazprom and the European Bank for Reconstruction and Development (EBRD).

As Figure 4.4 shows, gas production in the CIS has fallen about 55 mmtoe since 1990, mainly or wholly because of lack of markets. Russian consumption fell 20 mmtoe from 1990 to 1993; the rest of the CIS fell 35 mmtoe. Lower demand in Ukraine and Belarus was matched by a reduction in Russian imports from Turkmenistan and Uzbekistan so that Russian production was only 20–25 mmtoe lower.

Exports to the West increased slightly and exports to eastern Europe fell slightly.

Russian gas reserves would support levels of production which are higher by several orders of magnitude: 75% of the current 'proved' gas reserves – 26% of world proven gas reserves – occur in 20 uniquely large fields in Russia. Three of these are targeted for future development (two in the Yamal peninsula and one offshore the Barents Sea). Environmental considerations would affect costs and access. There are arrays of large and medium-sized undeveloped fields which are closer to the existing pipeline infrastructure in Siberia, and where development costs are expected to be lower. Development of a number of these fields would not only compensate for any decline in the Urengoy and Medvezhde fields but could support higher overall levels of production than at present.

There are also large potential resources, not on the scale of West Siberia, and not yet fully proved, in East Siberia, the Sakha republic, and offshore Sakhalin island. In contrast to the oil sector, there are no joint ventures with foreign companies in the gas sector, though some oil-producing joint ventures are also producers of gas on a small scale. Some of the large foreign oil projects (described below) will produce gas as well as oil.

As Figure 4.5 shows, some 70% of Russian gas production in 1994 went to the domestic market, including the operation of the gas system and stocks, 11% was exported to western Europe, 6% to central and eastern Europe, and 12% to the other CIS, net of imports from Turkmenistan. There are two consequences of this arithmetic. So long as the pipelines work, exports can be protected from fluctuations in production by relatively small adjustments to supplies to the domestic market. Conversely, a 7% fall in domestic demand would create the potential to increase exports to western Europe by 50%. Gazprom supplied 30% of Europe's gas consumption in 1993 (40% of the importing European countries' consumption).

Gas prices in Russia were substantially increased throughout 1995. By September, prices for industrial consumers were roughly at the equivalent to export netbacks (but many industrial customers were not paying their bills). It has been argued that continuing price reform alone will reduce domestic demand significantly and increase the availability of gas for export without

Figure 4.5 Disposition of Russian gas production

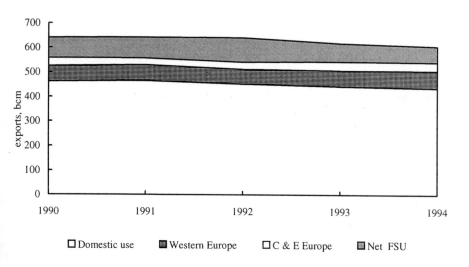

□ Domestic use   ▥ Western Europe   □ C & E Europe   ▩ Net FSU

Source: IEA (1995a).

further investment except in export transmission lines and, in the consuming sector, in meters, efficient appliances and equipment, and control systems to achieve efficiency).[4] The limit is more likely to be markets (see below) than investment in production. A survey of recent Russian projections of gas production for the year 2010[5] contrasts Gazprom projections of 40–50% increases above 1994 level with Ministry of Fuel and Energy projections of 20–27% increases above the 1994 level. On the importing side, most European countries expect an increase of the share of gas in their primary energy supply[6] and an increase in consumption of 50% (nearly 150 bcm). This necessarily involves increasing imports from Russia.

The Russia Energy Strategy envisages expansion of gas production of

---

[4]   See Stern (1995).
[5]   IEA (1995c), p. 426.
[6]   The IEA *Natural Gas Security Study* reports member country submissions of expected increases in the gas share of national primary energy demand by the year 2005 as follows: Germany 3%, UK 3%, Italy 9%, Austria 3%, Spain 6%, Portugal 8%.
[7]   IEA (1995a).

between 15% and 40% by the year 2010.[7] The rate of development will be determined by investment and the expansion of markets, rather than resource constraints. Export increases of 30–60%, as envisaged in the strategy, are possible, given markets and investment, from discovered reserves. The IEA Natural Gas Security study analysis of the competitiveness of Russian gas suggests that (for new West Siberian supplies to western Europe), Russian gas could be competitive with imports of LNG and with residual fuel oil delivered at $16–18 per barrel.

As gas prices to Russian consumers continue to be increased, demand may fall further, making additional export volumes available for the cost of expanding the export pipelines westward from the main consuming areas. In effect, the volume of gas exports to western Europe can be decided by the rate of investment in Russian supply and the pricing policies in the Russian domestic market – for both of which Gazprom is responsible.

The politics of Russian gas

The Russian gas industry has several features with strong political implications: the monopoly position of Gazprom; its dependence on transit through countries for exports to western Europe; its control over transit for other gas exporting countries in central Asia; and its policy of forward integration into its export markets – into the western European gas distribution 'club'.

The Gazprom monopoly

Ninety-five per cent of Russia's gas production is carried out by production associations contracted to Gazprom, which owns all of Russia's high-pressure transmission lines and infrastructure. Gazprom emerged from the remains of the former Soviet Gas Ministry (absorbed into the Soviet Ministry of Oil and Gas in 1989) during the period 1989–92. It took the form first of a 'concern', then of a joint-stock company (in 1992). Control over the local production associations was substantially increased during the restructuring of 1992. Distribution to final consumers and to industrial customers (which, however, Gazprom may also supply direct) is in the hands of some 600 distribution companies in which local and regional governments have shareholdings.[8] Gazprom (subject to government decree) sets the price at which it buys gas from the production associations and at which it sells gas to the distribution associations in Russia. Prices to producers have recently been set close to variable cost: Gazprom finances production capital expenditure from its margin.[9]

According to the IEA's survey of *Energy Policies of the Russian Federation* (1995a), Gazprom's selling prices within Russia are not adjusted for different transport costs, while those for other fuels such as coal and oil products have, since 1993, made such adjustment. The result has been a significant distortion of relative prices to the disadvantage of competing fuels (which depend largely on rail distribution). Industrial concerns pay higher prices than residential consumers (a significant cross-subsidy).

For exports, gas prices to western Europe are defined in hard currency, and governed by long-term international contracts of varying complexity which take into account the price of competing fuels (such as oil products) on the international market.

Gas prices to eastern European transit countries (see below) were rebated or relieved for certain volumes of production in payment for construction costs incurred in building the pipeline. The contracts which governed these arrangements have ended or are coming to an end, and new contracts, presumably following the west European model, have been or are being negotiated.

For former Soviet Union countries, prices prior to the collapse of the rouble zone were essentially Russian domestic prices. Since then, contractual prices have been negotiated, but payment of the new prices has often been in arrears or in default (the IEA reports the accrual of $1.8 bn arrears between January and October 1994). These arrears have largely been replaced by a series of rescheduling agreements and by extensive use of what amount to debt-for-equity swaps. By the same process Gazprom has become a major shareholder in the gas distribution

---

[8] In 1994, the central distribution organization Rosgazifikatsiya was decentralized into independent joint stock companies.

[9] For further information, see Kryukov and Moe (1996).

facilities in Belarus, but the problem remains a significant one within a complex of disputes about liabilities and assets divided between the successor states of the former Soviet Union.

It is difficult to imagine that the Gazprom monopoly will not come under pressure in the future, however well it served Russia in maintaining essential energy supplies and exports during the worst period of the transition from the central planning system. Ironically, the very steps taken to enable Gazprom to function effectively during the period of transition may make it more difficult for it to adapt to the eventual introduction of competition and decentralization which a further development of the market economy is likely to bring for reasons defined entirely by Russian interests: to increase efficiency, to reduce arbitrary redistribution of resources through central pricing and investment decisions, and to depoliticize the detailed management of an important industrial sector.

The transit questions

Russian gas exports, under Gazprom control and ownership, pass through Belarus and Ukraine en route for Central Europe, the Balkans and Turkey. Exports to Germany also pass through the Czech and Slovak Republics and Austria (see Map 2). A project to link the German and Russian systems by a new line through Poland will diversify Russia's export routes to some extent.

Gazprom, in its turn, controls the pipeline system by which Turkmenistan and Kazakhstan in the past exported gas to Russia and Ukraine. Russia used its control of the pipeline system to cut back Turkmenistan exports, and therefore production, in 1992–4 in order to protect markets for Russian gas. Later, Turkmenistan was forced to supply the non-paying Ukrainian market rather than export to western Europe. Disputes over payment for Russian gas delivered to Ukraine led at one point in December 1994 to a standstill in which Russian deliveries to Ukraine were suspended by Gazprom, and transit of Russian gas through Ukraine was blocked by the Ukraine government. Apart from the payments questions discussed above, there are also clear important access questions. Transit rights through Ukraine are guaranteed by a 1994 intergovernmental agreement.

Map 4.1 Russia and neighbours

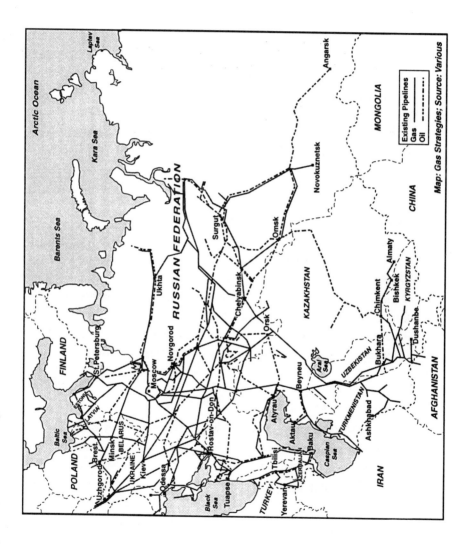

Map: Gas Strategies; Source: Various

Gazprom the international force

Finally, Gazprom has gone further than the newly created Russian integrated oil companies in extending its reach outside Russia and in resisting
the encroachment of other investors on its freedom to manage as a privatized joint-stock company.

Gazprom has set up 26 joint ventures with local or international companies in 13 countries, including most of its principal markets: Germany
(WINGAS, WIEH – for marketing outside Germany – ZEG, DITGAS),
France, Austria, Italy, Greece, Poland, Hungary and Finland. Most of these
are trading companies but all are vehicles for information and establishing
direct marketing relationships outside the traditional European gas inter-
mediaries. In Poland and Germany, Gazprom is also involved in pipeline
and facility construction and operation. It is a shareholder in the
UK–Continent interconnector project.

Oil production and projections

Compared with gas, oil production in Russia has declined dramatically; the
industry has been restructured and privatized in potentially competitive
vertically integrated oil companies; limited opportunities have been created for foreign investment in exploration and development. The development with foreign investment of oil potential in former Soviet Central
Asia, on the other hand, has been delayed by Russian claims over Caspian
oil resources and Russian control of effective transit routes for export.

Past achievement

The Russian oil industry has shown itself capable of remarkable effort.
Between 1965 and 1976 it completed the most extraordinary decade of
expansion of any industry operating under similar conditions anywhere in
the world, adding over 5 million barrels a day of capacity, mainly in
Siberia. During the same period Alaska added 1 million barrels a day in a
little under two years, the first 3 million of capacity came on in the North
Sea, and over 2 million was added in Mexico and Brazil. The reserve base

in these countries did not allow the continued expansion which was achieved in Russia. The reserve base in Saudi Arabia put that country in a different league: it added over 6 million barrels a day in the Eastern Province alone between 1965 and 1976. These figures do not capture the whole lead times of these projects. Nor do they reflect their costs. In Russia the early expansion was driven by quantitative rather than economic targets. The Russian expansion absorbed huge investment resources. Attempting to continue and maintain this growth through the 1980s absorbed an increasing share of Soviet investment resources.

The oil crisis

Russian oil production declined about 45% between 1987 and 1994 (as Figure 4.1 shows). The reasons for this decline have been extensively discussed in the technical and trade literature and by Russian spokesmen. A summary appears in the IEA's *Energy Policies of the Russian Federation*. Briefly, the peak production of the early 1980s had been achieved by various measures including intensive drilling and waterflooding of a relatively small number of large fields, of which Samotlor was the largest. Maintaining these levels of production was technically unsustainable; the decline could have been slowed by very large investment in pressure maintenance, but the funds for this were not available. Over most Russian fields, the drilling patterns had also been planned to meet centrally determined targets of numbers of wells, rather than optimized against the characteristics of the reservoir and the economics of drilling. Drill pipe was of a poor quality, so that wells were not often pumped at their drilled depth, and drilling tools did not achieve the depths known in the West. Horizontal drilling (introduced in the USA and the UK in the late 1980s) was not introduced in Russia.

The mismatching of technology with economics was combined with an acute shortage of funds in the last days of the Soviet Union, followed by a period of disorganization during the restructuring of the oil industry from 1989 to 1994. Not only was output from producing fields declining rapidly, but fields which had been identified by previous exploration were not being developed to supplement production.

Foreign funds began to flow in 1993 through a $799m World
Bank/EBRD credit programme. This was followed in 1994 by a variety of
US Export-Import Bank loans and credits which could increase to a limit of
$2 billion. Various semi-commercial credits have also been established.
However, to the extent that any of these credits pre-empt Russian oil export
earnings which would otherwise be available to service Russian sovereign
foreign debt, they meet objections from the multilateral agencies.

Price and tax reforms during 1995 (discussed below) also restored some
cash flow to an industry which had suffered exceptionally from the economic reforms: its access to state capital had been cut off but its output
prices had remained controlled while input prices had been liberalized.
Production in 1995 was only 100,000 bd (2%) below 1994, and is expected to be roughly the same in 1996.[10]

Foreign investment

Foreign equity – money without management – is Russia's preferred route
for foreign investment. Both Lukoil and Gazprom plan to market their
equity in Western financial markets. Foreigners can already buy their
shares on Russian stock exchanges.

In general, the equity shares available to foreigners are small and do not
involve control of strategy, budgets or operation. In the long run, as disclosure standards improve and shareholders' rights are more clearly protected, foreign portfolio investment in Russian oil companies and
Gazprom is likely to grow, attracted by Russia's resource potential and the
strength of a few large enterprises. Such foreign equity investment will
have a spin-off benefit for Russian investors because it will provide pressure for higher standards of financial disclosure, and for the resolution of
credit and economic restructuring problems. Higher standards of disclosure and financial structure for foreign investors will automatically be
available to domestic investors. Foreign portfolio investment could be an
important lever in moving major Russian energy enterprises towards acting as market-oriented economic agents. Enterprises which choose this
route will be preferred by Russian as well as foreign capital markets.

---

[10] IEA, *Oil Market Report*, 7 February 1996.

Joint ventures or 'joint enterprises' in working oilfields which are already producing have been the main routes for foreign investment in the oil sector so far. Direct foreign oil industry investment brought in about $1.7 bn to the beginning of 1995.[11] These are very small sums for a petroleum industry which invests about $90 bn annually outside the former communist areas.[12] Joint ventures or contracts with some 40 foreign partners currently supply about 5% of Russian production:[13] the majority of these producing ventures involve 'working over' – maintaining and enhancing production from existing operations rather than investment of capital in long-term future production.

The joint ventures are most affected by the current fluctuations of policy on prices, export allocations, and taxes. The number of joint ventures of this kind is not increasing. For foreign companies, the experience has generally been a learning rather than a profitable process. For US companies, there has been recourse to the 'Gore–Chernomyrdin' process[14] to resolve disputes affecting particular companies – for example, companies in joint ventures affected by the continual changes in export regulations and taxes experienced by foreign investors in the Russian oil sector.

Major new projects

Since the end of the Soviet Union in December 1995, and the resolution of the struggle about governmental process in December 1993, there has been considerable progress in setting up the necessary framework for foreign investment. Important steps relevant to energy were:

• The Federation Treaties of March 1992 stabilized the relationships between the Federal Russian governments and the republic, oblast and autonomous region governments.

---

[11] IEA (1995a).

[12] Estimate by Weaver (1994).

[13] Estimate in the *Russian Petroleum Investor*, June 1995.

[14] A joint committee headed by these two individuals to discuss matters of mutual economic interest. It is staffed on the US side through a special office in the State Department. Its agenda provides a mechanism for coordinating and prioritizing bilateral economic issues from the US and Russian perspectives.

- The Law on Foreign Investment (July 1991) provided basic rights of establishment and legal protection.
- The Law on Property (December 1991) created property rights for Russians and foreigners.
- The Law on Mineral Resources (February 1992) established federal ownership of underground resources, licensing procedures, and some rights of regional governments to revenue sharing.
- A Bankruptcy Law (March 1993), and the Civil Code (1994) provided basic protection of command enforceability of contracts.
- The Production Sharing Law (December 1995) substituted contracted production shares for taxation.

Production-sharing regimes are widely used outside Europe and North America and have proved resilient under changing price and costs regimes. The Russian law as passed has provisions which are not attractive to foreign investors: absence of international arbitration and freedom for the government to reopen clauses in the event of significant changes in circumstances, and the need for parliamentary (rather than government) approval of contracts for operations in offshore and (undefined) 'strategic' regions. However, in direction the law is a positive move and fills a role necessary for the development of a comprehensive framework for foreign investment.

Within this framework, or something evolved from it, are investments with foreign participation which lie in the future but which are likely to be producing post-2000. Four or five major projects (affecting about 11 bn bbls of reserves) are in an advanced stage of negotiation: production-sharing agreements, contingent on the passage of compatible legislation, have been concluded for two of them. There could be more, if more discovered but undeveloped reservoirs were opened to foreign participation. These projects are relatively unaffected by current prices, market access and tax fluctuations, except in so far as these are seen as an indicator of future policy and instability: the revenues lie in the 5–10 year future. The main capital expenditures await the adoption of satisfactory production–sharing laws, and related taxes, and the quality of the acreage released for licensing in new licensing rounds. These ventures are likely to be the main channels for future transfers of management and technology, and for foreign direct investment (totalling perhaps $3–5 bn annually) in oil and gas production.

Given the complexity of the projects and the lead times, and the current impasse on legislation, one could imagine about 1 mmbd of production, originating in these projects, around the turn of the century and perhaps as much again between the years 2000 and 2010. The foreign share (averaging say 50% at best) of these projects would be around 10% of Russian production, similar to the foreign share in US production today.

Future oil production

Assuming a steady improvement in the policy environment (prices, taxes, and permits), production in 2000 could be in the range 300 to 320 mmt. By 2010, assuming the current major foreign projects proceed,[15] 350 mmt or higher would be possible – roughly 1 mmbd above current levels. About half of this might be available from Sakhalin for export to the East Asian markets. Release of more undeveloped but discovered reserves for development by foreign-led consortia might raise this a further 25–50 mmt to 8 mmbd by 2010, if foreign participation led to the more rapid development of these fields (there are 50–60 large oilfields discovered but undeveloped in Russia: not all are necessarily viable)[16] but this is not on the current policy agenda.

Exports

The collapse of oil exports since 1990 means that gas is now the major petroleum export in energy terms, though for western Europe oil has recovered volume and overtaken it (1995 figures are similar to 1994). As Figure 4.6 shows, since 1990 supplies to the 'near abroad' have fallen, partly because the markets there have collapsed, partly because, as oil production collapsed, the burden of shortages was placed on the other republics, partly because, while the rouble zone remained in existence, the

---

[15] Projects in Sakhalin, Timen-Pechora, Priobskoya.
[16] See table provided by VNIICTEP in the *Petroleum Economist* (1994).

Figure 4.6 Russian gas and oil exports

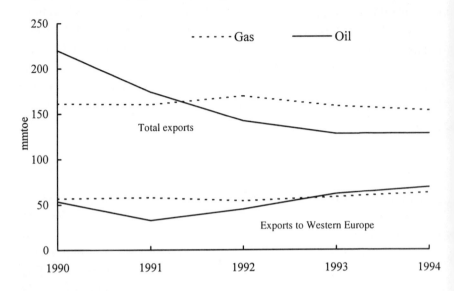

Source: IEA (1995a).

other republics were creating roubles in order to pay for the imports. Exports to eastern Europe followed a somewhat similar pattern.

Russian oil exports to the West in 1994 and 1995 were limited by the export capacity of the terminals at the ports of Novorossiysk and Ventspils. Spare capacity on the pipelines to eastern Europe was not useful since demand there had fallen, there were payments difficulties, and transit tariffs had been increased. Some production was probably shut in rather than exported under these conditions. There are plans to expand the terminal at Novorossiysk and to build a new line to the Baltic. All Russian oil producers are anxious to increase their capacity to export to western European markets rather than depend on demand in the CIS or in Poland, Hungary and the Czech Republic. There is currently significantly excess pipeline capacity to these markets, but their demand is expected to recover slowly.

Consumption trends are very uncertain. Economic recovery should correlate closely with improved energy efficiency, and the availability of gas (see below) should lead to further substitution of gas for oil in industry.

Demand for oil by 2010 could easily be in the range 4–5 mmbd, less than 1 mmbd above current levels.[17] Russia is therefore likely to maintain its oil export capacity to Europe and the 'near abroad' of around 3 mmbd at or above present levels for the next decade at least, while successful agreements to develop the Sakhalin projects could bring perhaps an additional 0.5 mmbd or more to the East Asian market.

Central Asian oil and gas[18]

Production potential

The five Central Asian successor states to the former Soviet Union are reported to have about 20 bn barrels of proved oil deposits and 7 trillion cubic metres of proved gas. The offshore Caspian is reported as containing 10–15 bn barrels of undiscovered oil.[19] Oil production was, however, only 630,000 bd in 1993 (exports around 70,000 bd to the West, and 50,000 bd for CIS refineries were allocated for 1994), and gas production 298 cubic metres per day (of which about 90 were exported outside the CIS).

Kazakhstan and Azerbaijan are, the principal resource-rich, economically poor, relatively underpopulated countries which have shown an eagerness to develop their resources. Successful resource development would strengthen their economic independence. Developments in these CIS states depend on foreign investment – since there is no possibility that the major projects required could be financed domestically. They also need foreign technology – since they are mainly in deeper water than the former Soviet industry had operated in.

Azerbaijan and Kazakhstan have followed active policies of encouraging foreign participation in oil and gas development, though the history of individual projects has fluctuated with changes of government and the commercial composition of the foreign partnerships involved. The projects currently planned (for which production-sharing agreements have

---

[17] See Crandall (1994), for a typical forecast.

[18] For a comprehensive review of the export potential and related pipeline issues, see Ottar Skagen, IEA Staff Paper dated 15 June 1995.

[19] 'Russia Insists on a Slice of the Action', *Petroleum Economist*, March 1995, pp. 14–15.

been either signed with identified foreign companies or signed and ratified by the current administrations) could support an additional 1.5 mmbd
of oil production.[20]

For the five countries together, World Bank studies suggest a possibility of net oil exports from the region of 1.5 to 1.9 mmbd and net gas exports
of 95–135 bcm by 2010, if export routes do not prove a constraint, development takes place as planned, and local consumption grows moderately.

Transit and access

Current existing export routes are either to the Russian market or through
Russia to the port of Novorossiysk for export of oil and for transit or
exchange through the Gazprom system for the export of gas. For
Azerbaijan, there is the possibility of moving a small volume of oil, by
connecting to existing lines to Batum in Georgia. After prolonged negotiations agreement appeared to have been reached by the AIOC consortium,
which includes Lukoil, that 'early oil' production from the consortium's
investments in Azerbaijan will be exported through both the Russian and
Georgian routes.[21] A decision will be taken in 1997 regarding expansion of
these routes or alternatives to them. In the medium to long term, there may
be scope for increasing demand within the region, for export to neighbouring areas of Russia, to Ukraine and to Turkey. There have been proposals for exports to northern Iran to be exchanged for Iranian exports in
the Gulf. In the longer run, and for significant increases in volumes of oil
export, there has been active competition between various projects. Of
these the most active have been the following:

- The Caspian Pipeline Consortium Scheme, aimed mainly at providing an
  export route for oil from Kazakhstan to the Russian port of Novorossiysk
  on the Black Sea. Progress on this scheme, based on expanding existing
  lines, has been hampered by commercial conflicts arising from the dif-
  fering partnerships in the pipeline and the producing areas and by the

---

[20] Estimate by Rase (1995).
[21] *Financial Times*, 28 February 1996.

necessity to secure Russian participation and commitment, which in June 1996 stood at 44%. Azerbaijan oil exports could also flow to Novorossiysk through the construction new lines on existing routes through Dagestan and Chechnia (both constituents of the Russian Federation). Exports from Novorossiysk – to the extent they were not absorbed in Black Sea markets would need to be shipped through the Bosphorus or to bypass it by a landline such as that proposed through Bulgaria and Greece.

- Various schemes promoted by Botas, the Turkish state pipeline company, aimed at developing a new pipeline to carry Azeri oil to the port of Ceyhan in the Eastern Mediterranean (which is also an export terminal for Iraq). This route would have three advantages for Turkey: pipeline construction and tariff revenue, the enlargement of its port of Ceyhan, and avoidance of the environmental risks associated with greatly increased shipping of oil out of the Black Sea through the crowded Bosphorus channel. Ceyhan could be supplied by various routes, involving transit through Georgia, Armenia or Iran – there is no frontier between Turkey and Azerbaijan. Gas could also be brought to Turkey, an expanding market.

- The expansion of the existing pipeline route from Baku in Azerbaijan to Batumi in Georgia. Conceptually, Kazakhstan exports could also be brought into this route by expansion of existing lines.

- Proposals by Iran to connect Caspian oil to the Iranian pipeline system for direct shipment (or oil swaps for shipment) to Asian markets have been made. Whatever their economic merit, consideration of them has been blocked by the US administration, clearly indicating that it would regard participation in such schemes as giving support to the Iranian oil industry and subject to US sanctions. Iranian participation in the Azerbaijan International Oil Consortium (AIOC) was blocked by the USA, though the Iranian National Oil Company has been admitted as a commercial partner to the Shak Deniz project in Azerbaijan, in which there are no US companies directly involved. Iran is a Caspian littoral state and will have some territorial rights there. This is relevant because the international status of the Caspian is in dispute.[22]

Russia claims that the Caspian, as an inland sea, is subject to joint

---

[22] For a review, see Henn-Jüri Uibopuu (1995).

agreements on development. The other former Soviet states take the view that the Caspian should be allocated, like an open sea, into offshore zones of economic influence. Russia has also claimed that environmental protection requires Caspian developments to be coordinated, if not exactly centrally planned.[23]

The geopolitical cocktail

It is clear that all these development and export options have strong political implications: through them Russia may seek to control, or at least intermediate, the development of independent sources of wealth and foreign interdependence for the central Asian states and Azerbaijan. The relations of these states with each other, with Turkey and Iran, and with the Western countries providing the investment partners, is also involved.

Russia's interest must be to minimize the interest of others, whether Western countries from which the foreign oil and gas companies come, or neighbouring countries such as Turkey and Iran which have both historical territorial interests and interests in kindred populations of co-religionists in the area. If Russia can prevent neither the petroleum developments nor the incorporation of these independent states into a federal relationship, its interest therefore requires that it provides the transit routes and legal support for the developments to proceed through its territory and through other CIS states, but at a pace and on terms over which it exercises influence.

Russia may pursue its objectives by a variety of means: through its legal arguments about the status of the Caspian; through its consent for pipeline developments and port developments in its territory, and through political and economic pressures on the states concerned with which it shares an agenda of issues: the position of Russian minorities in these states and minorities from these states in Russia; trade and financial relationships; mutual security and the defence of the frontiers of the former Soviet Union, and internal stability. Russian enterprises may have

---

[23] For a further discussion of the issues involved in the various pipeline options see Roberts (1996).

Figure 4.7 Russian coal use 1994

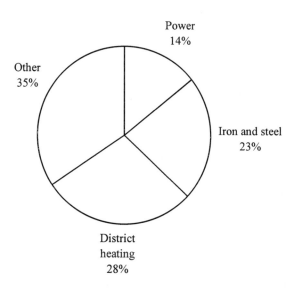

Source: IEA (1995a).

a connecting role. Lukoil, a leading Russian integrated oil company, is a participant (12.5%) in the AIOC and in the Tengiz project (10%) in Kazakhstan. Gazprom will be involved in any realistic gas export scheme involving the use of its system.

Non-petroleum energy
Coal

Coal accounted for just under 20% of Russian primary energy consumption in 1994, and Russian coal consumption was just under 6% of world coal consumption. Given the large coal resources, the existence of producing areas dependent on coal production, and the commitment of existing consumers (shown in Figure 4.7), coal is likely to remain a significant energy source, though at present it is in difficulties.

The international importance of Russia's coal industry is indirect: the social and political difficulties and cost of maintaining the industry in its present form, or of restructuring it, will be a burden on the Russian economy and a challenge to the authority of the policies of the Russian government. The coal industry remains in 1996 dependent on subsidies from a 'sector fund' and the weak mines are protected by the results of the strong under the common ownership of Rosugol.

The coal industry's current problems are in part the result of bad policy sequencing: the former Soviet rail tariffs (which equalized coal prices across the Soviet Union) have been replaced by cost- and distance-related tariffs, while gas tariffs have not. Under these half-reformed market conditions a large part of the former industrial and power market for coal has been dramatically disadvantaged relative to gas. Further competitive problems have been created by the relatively slow increase of gas and oil prices to industrial customers.

The size and location of coal markets and production under the future market conditions is difficult to determine. However, as indicated earlier, Russia's gas production potential is capable of supporting a significant switch from coal without affecting medium- or long-term gas export potential.

Electricity

The central electricity distribution system and the nuclear generating system remain separately centralized. Regional distribution companies and some generating capacity are decentralized to regional and potentially private ownership. In the long run it is possible to imagine an electricity industry with privately or municipally owned distribution, and with foreign participation in independent power production as in other countries. At this point international issues may arise in connection with foreign investment.

Nuclear

In 1994 Russia generated about 4% of the world's nuclear power and derived about 4% of its primary energy from nuclear sources. The international importance of the Russian nuclear industry derives from other factors: the possibility of 'another Chernobyl' either in Russia or in one of the Russian-built reactors in Eastern Europe or the 'near abroad'; the collapse of an ambitious nuclear expansion programme, which leaves the nuclear construction industry with excess building capacity and active in seeking nuclear construction contracts abroad; the management of the nuclear fuel cycles, including the stock of plutonium released from the run-down of the nuclear weapons arsenal, and the long-term storage of spent fuel (currently stored on site).

In 1992 Minatom published a plan which envisaged a 'period of consolidation and renovation' to the year 2000, focused on making existing reactors safe and completing a second fast breeder reactor. In the longer term, nuclear generating capacity would be doubled and a series of fast breeder reactors, linked with reprocessing, developed to close a large part of the fuel cycle. Development on these lines, even if technically feasible, would require massive investment. Minatom, a state enterprise separate from the electricity system RAOES, is in no position to fund it, and it is not easy to see any credible tariff structure which would permit it to be funded from Minatom's own resources.

Foreign assistance has so far been focused on technical studies and urgent safety projects for existing reactors. For the limited foreign aid available Russia must compete with Ukraine, other near abroad countries, and eastern Europe, all of which have urgent nuclear safety problems whether existing stations are kept running (and stations under construction are completed) or not.

Any significant foreign funds, as might be considered by the West, would probably be linked to an agreement by Russia on effective closer control of military and ex-military plutonium stockpiles, and on the transfer of civil nuclear technology to countries which have not signed the Nuclear Non-proliferation Treaty or, having signed, are not convincing in their compliance with it. Such agreement by Russia would significantly reduce its foreign policy options *vis-à-vis* Iran, Iraq, Pakistan and North Korea, all of which are potential clients for Russian civil nuclear technology and all of which are interested in developing nuclear weapons capabilities.

There is thus a suite of unresolved internal and external issues connected with Russia's nuclear industry which cannot be resolved by Russia alone (for financial reasons: its technical capability is not in doubt), and cannot be resolved in cooperation with other nuclear countries except at great financial cost.

The Russian political context

As Winston Churchill famously remarked: 'I cannot forecast to you the action of Russia. It is a riddle wrapped in a mystery inside an enigma. But perhaps there is a key. It is the Russian national interest.'[24]

The Russian economy is in transition from its place in the Soviet Union's centrally planned past to a future in which policy is exercised over a different geographic territory, governed by democratic institutions, within the dynamics of a market economy driven by individual, rather than collective, property rights and choices. It is over ten years since the rising Mikhail Gorbachev and some of his peers apparently said to one another 'We cannot go on like this'. The transition from a failing, centrally planned Soviet empire to a rising, decentralized economy in Russia probably passed through its low point between 1991 and 1993, when the territory of the Soviet Union was divided between successor states, when the Moscow and other governments' efforts to sustain the central distribution of goods and services of the economy collapsed, and when hyperinflation threatened to destroy the essential medium of exchange.

Waving not drowning

By comparison to the uncertainties which prevailed in the last days of the Soviet Union, and the earliest days of the independent Russian Republic, many questions have been resolved: the boundaries between Russia and the republics; the relations between the Russian Federated Republic and its constituents;[25] the broad balance of power between the President and the Duma; the separation of most industrial enterprises from the ministerial

---

[24] Winston S. Churchill, broadcast, 1939. Quoted in *Oxford Dictionary of Quotations* (OUP, 1950).
[25] With the important exception of Chechenia, at the time of writing.

budgets, and the privatization of the great part of the economy; the establishment of internal free trade and the use of money as an internal medium of exchange and accountability;[26] an outline system of property and contractual rights; and a macroeconomic structure and policy of public sector finance, monetary control, foreign exchange, and a private banking system which is broadly recognizable to the mandarins of the IMF. In a historically unique achievement, these structures have been introduced at the same time as democratic institutions expressing the results of consecutive free elections.[27]

Though the range of macro uncertainties about Russia has narrowed steadily since 1993, much remains uncertain today by comparison with the relative stability of US, Japanese or European political and economic structures. A methodology is needed for thinking about these uncertainties.

Sands of change

In this surge of change it is not surprising that policies have developed erratically. The Russian polity and economy have been moving forward like a football team crossing quicksand. Each player seems continuously to be in trouble. The economic reformers cannot move far if the territorial control is slipping (as when the Soviet Union was breaking up) or when policy-making is blocked by constitutional conflict (as during the period preceding the parliamentary election of 1993). Playing for political stability and democratic progress in turn requires economic results which are difficult to deliver when one economic system has broken down (as the Soviet planning system did in 1990–1) and its substitute is not yet up and running. The team cannot play as team until all the players have got through to the other side. The important questions for the spectators and those who have money riding on the result are whether all the players are moving in the same direction and whether they are heading towards firm ground. Only when the whole team has got across will it be reasonable to expect them to play a decent game. Since the parliamentary elections of 1993, and the pres-

---

[26] Modified by a continuing, but diminishing, problem of late and defaulted payments.

[27] For more information see the Post-Soviet Business Forum publications, RIIA, London.

idential elections of 1996, it can be argued that all the elements of change have been moving in the same direction it is extremely difficult to see that the decentralization of the economy can be reversed (though some features of the privatization of key enterprises may be revised); within a period of 5–10 years 'the team will have got to the other side' and there will be an effective, property-based, market-managed economy of the type described by Daniel Yergin and Thane Gustavson in their 'Chudo' scenario for 'Russia 2010'.[27] Such an economy would renew Russia's capacity as a great world power. The Russian people and state would have overcome the challenges of change and not been overwhelmed by them.

Obscurities ahead

There are areas where, in 1996, direction and progress are less clear and less encouraging:

- Criminality and corruption, especially in the muddy interface between government, legitimate enterprise and organized.
- Territorial integrity, challenged by Chechenia: so long as the challenge is limited to Chechenia, it may not seriously disrupt the process of change in Russia as a whole.
- External relations: Russian foreign policy since 1991 may not have been unsuccessful for a country which had lost important parts of its territory, its economic capability, and most of its reputation for power and might. But there are still challenges which are clearly unresolved; especially the precise relationship (and frontier) with NATO.
- The degree of independence of various countries in the 'near abroad', of which Ukraine is of the greatest absolute importance and the Trans-Caucasus and Central Asian states are of particular interest from the point of view of energy production.
- The bundle of nuclear issues described above, in which the key questions are who will pay to put Russia's civil nuclear industry on a safe course, and how the external issues relating to the export of nuclear technology will be handled.

---

[27] Yergin and Gustavson (1993).

Conclusions for the new geopolitical agenda

For world energy prospects there are three important themes: change within Russia, change within other CIS countries critical to energy, and the relations between Russia and other countries.

Change within Russia

The analysis above suggests that the continuing transition towards a market economy in Russia is progressively presenting a more coherent policy framework for internal and external investment and trade, and the integration of the Russian energy markets and enterprises in the internal markets and financial system, where some of them will play a significant part. There are two principal exceptions to this trend:

- The monopoly power, independence and importance of Gazprom. This may at some future time be challenged for internal Russian reasons. It presents significant problems for the west European gas markets and industry.
- The nuclear industry, where Russia faces immense costs in making existing reactors safer, developing and constructing plants of safer and more economic design, and strengthening safety and security aspects of the storage of spent fuel and ex-military plutonium.

Relations with the 'near abroad'

The countries of the near abroad are important to Russia for many reasons: the presence of large populations of ethnic Russians in most of these countries, their strategic importance on Russia's borders, and the possibility that some of those bordering western Europe may move towards a defence relationship with NATO which would secure a higher degree of practical independence from Russia than would otherwise be possible. The dependence of these countries on Russian gas and oil supplies (and their current reluctance to pay for them) is very high. Some of them – notably Ukraine – are also critical transit countries for Russian oil and gas exports to the rest of Europe.

There are also energy dimensions of interdependence between Russia and the Central Asian 'near abroad'. Kazakhstan, Azerbaijan and Turkmenistan would find it very difficult to develop their offshore Caspian resources for export without Russian support: as already noted, the status of the Caspian is in doubt. Russia offers nearby markets and feasible transit routes for export. The USA has blocked consideration of export routes through Iran, if even they were economic. Export routes through Turkey can easily be put second, on economic grounds, to the development of existing routes through Russia and Georgia.

However, the prosperity of the near abroad continues to have strategic significance for Russia: impoverished independence in the near abroad could open the way for foreign influence in those countries and could lead to pressure on expatriate Russian populations – and economic migration to Russia. Energy projects in these countries, with Russian commercial participation, and using Russian territory or carrying Russian petroleum, can serve these wider Russian interests. They would involve cooperation, rather than confrontation, with rival interests as a medium for achieving Russian objectives.

Relations with other countries

Energy features on Russia's agenda with three principal areas of the 'far abroad':

- The USA, because of that country's interest in investment opportunities for its oil and gas companies in Russia and the Caspian countries and (a totally different US constituency) because of the problems associated with the Russian nuclear industry and its security and foreign policy implications.
- Western Europe, because of Russia's importance as a gas supplier, the monopolistic nature of that supply; and the further dependence which accession of eastern European countries would bring to the EU.
- East Asia, where the development of eastern Siberia's petroleum resources could add significantly to East Asian supply options and create growing markets in eastern Russia for East Asian products and services.

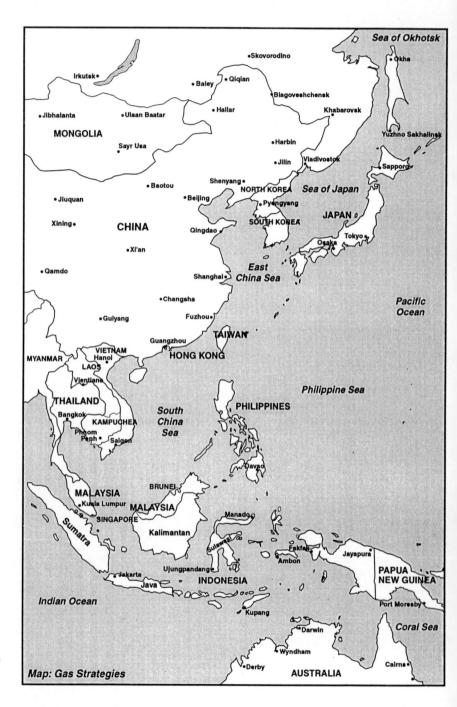

Map 5.1 Asia

Map: Gas Strategies

Chapter 5
East Asia

Introduction

East Asian energy matters to the world for three reasons:

- The size and growth of the region's energy demand: already nearly a quarter of world primary energy consumption, more than the European Union and soon probably as much as the United States. East Asian choices will affect world energy markets and world energy security. Investment in East Asian energy projects will provide good business – mainly for East Asians, but also for foreign investors with technology.
- East Asia's different mix of fuels: more than either Europe or the USA, it depends for its energy supplies on domestic coal (for China) and oil imported from the Middle East (for Japan and Korea). In the longer term (around 2010) there could be a major diversification of energy supplies: local nuclear programmes are set to grow irrespective of nuclear moratoriums elsewhere in the world. Growth of gas consumption depends on massive, dedicated cross-border investments for importing gas by pipeline from eastern Russia and in expanding and diversifying the supply of LNG.
- The continuing major role of governments in energy choices. However, regional institutions for resolving conflicts or promoting cooperation are weak, and political conflicts potentially affecting energy projects are many. Cross-border energy projects are exposed to disputes and tensions between countries in the region: border disputes, the integration of Taiwan in China, the reunification of Korea, and the political events which may accompany such developments.

In short, East Asia is a region where 'energy policy' still matters, and where some of its key issues are entwined in large regional and internation-

al political issues. Building understanding of these issues into global energy
and political thinking – into the 'new geopolitics' – is an important task for
the future. The mechanics and politics of securing reliable energy supplies
across borders may contribute to wider political and aconomic cooperation.

This chapter describes:

- the definition and main characteristics of the region;
- the economic phenomenon of its high growth and investment rates;
- the related energy demand and energy efficiency trends and their
  uncertainties;
- the fuel mix generated by sectoral demand and the different availability
  of local supplies;
- the outlook for energy supply within the region;
- the resulting regional trade and market structure;
- the international political and institutional setting.

Definition of the region

All definitions in Asia are compromises. For this study, 'East Asia' means
the area bounded by (and excluding) Russia to the north, the USA to the
east, Australasia to the south, and India, Pakistan, Bangladesh and
Myanmar to the west. It thus includes the 'sumo wrestler' economies of
China, Japan and Korea as well as the members of the Association of
Southeast Asian Nations (ASEAN). The excluded countries[1] are important
in their own right. Some (such as the USA, Russia and Australia) have
energy and geopolitical links and interests in 'East Asia': which are discussed. Ten of the fourteen political entities in the region account for virtually all the energy consumption.[2]

The ten energy-important countries of East Asia differ widely in size, population, and stages of economic development: In terms of population,
growth, and economic and energy weight, the 'heavyweights' or 'sumos' are

---

[1]   The term 'countries' is used here for convenience and is not intended to carry political
connotations.
[2]   Japan, China (with Hong Kong and Taiwan), Indonesia, the Republic of Korea,
Malaysia, the Philippines, Singapore and Thailand. The other four are Cambodia, Laos,
North Korea and Vietnam.

China (which with Hong Kong and Taiwan accounts for 45% of the regional energy consumption), Japan (25% of regional energy consumption), the Republic of Korea, and Indonesia. Malaysia, the Philippines, Singapore, Taiwan and Thailand have smaller populations, and most of their economies have enjoyed more rapid rates of growth in more open or opening economies, and more growth in foreign investment. There is a common economic culture of high savings, priority given to education, and export-oriented strategies, but there is no comparable commonality in political cultures and no dominant constitutional model.

Most of the Southeast Asian countries, including Indonesia, are parties to ASEAN, and various combinations of countries are parties to wider political and economic associations. There is in the region no equivalent of the European Union, and no mechanism for promoting a single market (beyond ASEAN free trade), or common currency. The absence of these institutions does not appear to prevent rapid economic growth, nor the advance in all the countries concerned of economic liberalization (including the removal of tariff barriers), increasing transparency of markets, and the withdrawal of the state from previously state-managed economic activities. APEC is emerging as a forum for discussion of economic subjects and includes countries in East Asia as well as the USA, Canada, and countries bordering the South Pacific. An Energy Committee of APEC was established in 1995, based in Japan. Its activities at present are focused on compiling statistical and descriptive information rather than developing policy analysis.

In a different dimension and most critically, there is no security or defence pact within the region. As in Europe, however, the USA and Russia have intervened in the past to challenge the growth of a dominant regional military power, and (with varying success) to induce or impose political and economic institutions in countries subsequently associated with them. As in Europe, political vacuums have been created by the collapse of Russian power during the past five years. In East Asia, the projection of Chinese power is growing: the incorporation of Hong Kong in 1997, the assertion of territorial claims over the Spratly Islands, and a more assertive stance towards Taiwan. As in Europe and the Middle East, the effective guarantor of national security in some key countries is the USA through mutual security pacts and (in the case of Japan and the Republic of Korea), a military presence.

Economic phenomena
Growth

There is a general expectation that countries in East Asia will continue to achieve higher rates of economic growth than their counterparts in developed and developing countries elsewhere, because of the combination of factors mentioned above and in particular because of high rates of capital invested, financed by domestic saving. High and sustained rates of economic growth are not new to East Asia. They were achieved in Japan over several decades. In the past fifteen years a number of countries (the 'Tigers') have taken the high-growth road, and economic reforms in China are moving the world's most populous country in the same direction.

Figure 5.1 shows that East Asia as region has outperformed the world average both in per capita and absolute economic growth. Within East Asia, the high-income countries, notably Japan, have outperformed high-income countries elsewhere, and the low- and middle- income countries have outperformed Japan.

There are many possible explanations for the economic success of East Asian countries: culture, policy, stability, in varying, changing and often contrasting forms, combining differently for different countries at different times. The present dynamic seems to require:

- continuing freedom from international conflict in the region;
- politics favourable to economic reform and liberalization continuing in China and the newly industrializing countries;
- continuation of the opening of multilateral trade, particularly within the region.
- continuing relatively free (and increasingly freer) flows of investment and technology.

These are probably necessary conditions for continuing high economic growth in East Asia. There is a simpler and more operational requirement: continuing high rates of investment.

Figure 5.1 Percentage annual growth in GDP, 1980–93

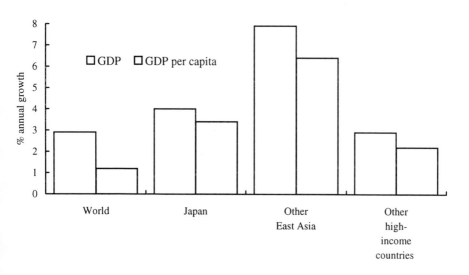

Note: 'Other high-income countries': high-income countries are as defined by the World Bank Atlas method: 1993 GDP per capita exceeds $8,626. Japan, Singapore, Hong Kong, and Brunei are high income countries in East Asia. The 'Other high-income countries' on the graph are the rest of the OECD (except Mexico), Israel, Kuwait, the UAE, Qatar, Greenland, Cyprus, Andorra, San Marino and a number of small island states and entities which are financial centres.
Source: World Bank (1995).

Investment

High rates of investment have been part of the East Asian economic phenomenon, for Japan and the other high-income countries as well as for China and the Tigers. These have in turn been supported by high rates of domestic saving, as Figure 5.2 shows. The high rates of investment generate future expectations of continuing future high rates of growth. Gross domestic investment in East Asian countries grew annually from 1980 to 1993 by nearly 10% outside Japan and by 5.5% in Japan (compared with 2.5% in the USA, 4% in the UK and less than 1% in Latin America).

Figure 5.2 Investment and savings, 1993

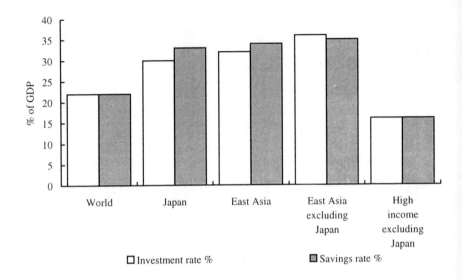

□ Investment rate %   ▨ Savings rate %

Source: World Bank (1995).

Foreign investment

For some East Asian countries, the high rates of investment currently use significant long-term foreign resources in the form of debt, direct investment, equity investment and (to a smaller degree) grants. In others, foreign funds are important at the margin, but not structurally. Countries with high rates of savings have unusual structural freedom to determine their own economic priorities. This does not mean that particular projects, regions or sectors in these countries cannot be 'short of capital' because of policy or market imperfections, but that these allocation problems are potentially soluble within national priorities. Countries with a high inflow of foreign resources have more exposure to international market conditions and opinion. (See figure 5.3.)

For most East Asian countries, foreign capital is available from a variety of sources: foreign direct investors have no special leverage when capital is available from foreign equity investors as well as long-term loans to the state or state agencies. Countries can choose: China has chosen to admit

Figure 5.3 Foreign resources in total investment, 1993

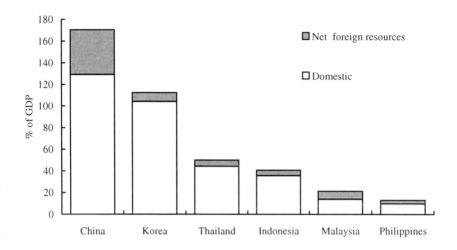

Source: World Bank (1995).

foreign direct investment. Korea has so far preferred the equity route, reserving most of its industrial and energy sectors for Korean companies, as Figure 5.4 shows. The recent decades of high growth in investment of domestic and foreign savings have also been periods in which, geopolitically, the region has been for the most part both stable and peaceful. The longer history of the past fifty years, while Europe was at peace, includes for East Asia the wars of independence, the confrontation between Indonesia and Malaysia, and the Korean and Vietnam wars.

Foreign investment in energy

There are large differences between the East Asian countries in the degree to which foreign direct investment is involved in the energy sector. In Indonesia, Malaysia, Thailand and Brunei, foreign partners invest in and operate oil and gas production investments, generally under production-sharing contracts in which the foreign company has a 50% share at most.

Figure 5.4 Sources of foreign funds, 1993

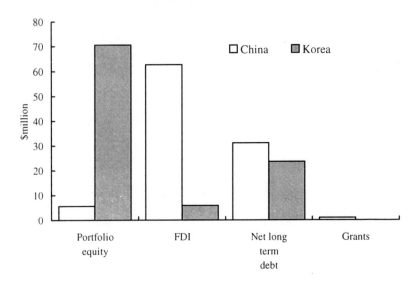

Source: World Bank (1995).

Such contracts are available in China, but the tracts allocated to foreign partners over the past decades have yielded few significant exploration successes. In oil refining and marketing, foreign participation varies from over 90% in Singapore, the international entrepôt, through 40–50% in Thailand, Malaysia and the Philippines, to 20% in Japan and slightly less in Korea – in both countries through joint ventures. There are projects for joint-venture refineries in China and for a joint-venture export refinery in Indonesia. In Indonesia, foreign companies invest directly, often in partnership with local companies, in coal and oil production, but not in refining and distributing oil products for the domestic market.

The power generation and gas distribution sectors are in private-sector (Japanese) hands in Japan. In China, different state-owned corporations (China National Petroleum Corporation, China National Offshore Oil Corporation) operate the onshore and offshore petroleum industry, with foreign joint ventures in certain areas. Power generation in China is decentralized, and the possibility exists for foreign investment in power plants.

While foreign international companies have limited and often low shares of energy investments in East Asia, there are strong local state companies in all sectors in China, and in the power and petroleum sectors in Indonesia and Malaysia. Local private-sector companies dominate the oil sector and power sector in Japan and Korea. Some of these companies are active outside their own borders: Korean refiners are moving into China. Japanese companies have been active internationally in exploration and production ventures for over two decades: just over 10% of Japanese oil imports originate from ventures in which Japanese companies have an interest.

Coexistence of state and private-sector companies is the rule in most East Asian countries, as well as strong central government influence over major strategic decisions, such as fuel choice and choice of trading partner countries for major energy supplies.

Energy consumption

Primary energy consumption is expected to grow at higher rates in East Asia than elsewhere, though more slowly than economic growth, especially in the wealthier countries such as Japan, which has achieved one of the greatest improvements in the use of energy in the world. Decades of high rates of economic growth brought East Asian's share of world energy consumption to just over 20% in 1994. It already consumes almost 30% more energy than the EU, and will probably overtake the USA before the year 2000. Even without Japan, the rest of East Asia is already almost as large an energy market as the EU, as Figure 5.5 shows.

Projections of demand

Most forecasters believe that the region will continue to be the fastest growing energy market in the world for some decades for the following reasons:

- The expectation that the Chinese economy will continue to grow at rates between 6% and 10%. Despite continuing rapid improvements in energy intensity this points to energy demand growth in the 4–7% range.

Figure 5.5 Primary energy consumption

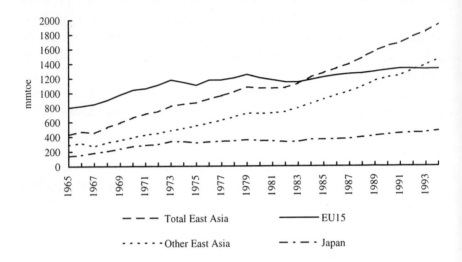

Source: *BP Statistical Review* (1995).

- Continuing growth in Japanese energy demand at over 1%. This assumes that (despite relatively flat oil and gas prices) energy saving and efficiency, and the growth of renewable energy, will achieve government objectives, rather than continue to fall short.
- Continuing rapid growth (5% and over) in most or all of the ASEAN countries, the Republic of Korea, and Taiwan.
- A continuing rapid expansion of the electricity sector: probably over 5% per year in the region. The forces generating this are complex: in many countries, electricity prices have been held down by cheap capital and even subsidies, but supplies have grown more slowly than demand. The higher prices necessary to finance expansion (whether in private or state hands) might dampen demand growth: fuel costs could also increase as more remote sources of gas are brought into supply. There is a wide range of uncertainty – mainly downward from past trends – about the likely growth and composition of the electricity sector's fuel demand.

- The expectation that transport demand will also grow more rapidly than the average – perhaps 7% per annum in the region as a whole.

In all countries in the region, oil demand is projected to grow more rapidly than total energy demand, because of shifts in economic structure, giving energy demand growth of about 5% on average.

Increasing efficiency

The link between GDP growth and energy consumption is changing in East Asia, as everywhere in the world, and the degree of change differs between countries. There are several reasons for these differences:

- In some countries, non-commercial energy is important (but it is normally excluded from international energy statistics). As an economy grows, non-conventional supplies often fail to grow, so that *commercial* energy appears to grow fast relative to GDP.
- The structure of the economy changes:[3] during the development of heavy and energy-intensive industries, energy consumption grows rapidly, and grows rapidly again when automotive personal and freight transport grows.
- Urbanization increases commercial energy consumption in the household sector, but that growth may lag behind the industrial sector and eventually faces saturation factors.
- Energy prices also play a part: in much of East Asia prices have been distorted from international prices by price controls, market regulation, state enterprise pricing policies, and subsidies to the power sector.[4]
- In East Asia the connection between growth in GDP and growth in energy consumption varies widely, Japan performing better and Korea and China worse than countries such as the USA, UK and France, as Figure 5.6 shows.

---

[3] See Schipper (1995).
[4] For one among many discussions, see World Bank (1993).

Figure 5.6 Growth in GDP per unit of energy, 1970–1993

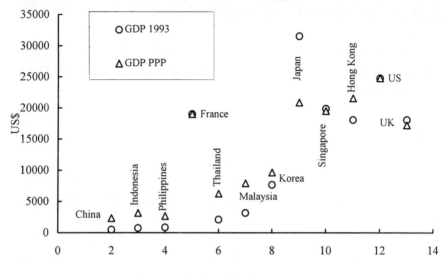

Increase GDP/kgoe 1970-93

Source: World Bank (1995).

In very broad terms, there does appear to be a connection between the level of income and growth in GDP per unit of energy, as Figure 5.6 shows. The vertical axis measures the multiples (2 = double) of increased GDP per kgoe of energy consumed, 1971–80. Very broadly, the higher the level of GDP per person (calculated for 1993), the more the growth of GDP has exceeded the growth of energy consumption over recent decades. The same relationship appears to hold when the GDP figure is adjusted for purchasing power parity (PPP). (It can be argued that, for quantitative purposes, it is the adjusted PPP figure that matters.[5]) The inclusion of the USA and the UK on the chart shows that the broad trend is not different in East Asian countries from elsewhere.

This is what one would expect from long-run trends in which energy consumption grows less fast than GDP for the kind of reason described

---

[5]   See Siddiqui (1994).

above.[6] The countries with high levels of income in 1993 have, in general, achieved those levels through longer histories of high growth during which differences between GDP and energy growth have accumulated. The implication is to give some credibility to forecasts which suggest a widening gap between GDP growth and energy consumption as countries get wealthier. Energy demand forecasting for rapidly growing economies is very difficult: simple extrapolations will not do.

Uncertainties in demand forecasts

A large part of future demand in rapidly growing economies will be determined by developments which have not yet occurred, in contrast to mature economies where the greater part of energy-using capital stock for, say, the next fifteen years is already in place. The forecaster for the rapidly growing economy is not protected by inertia. A series of extremely difficult questions present themselves:

- Will the rates of economic growth change, and if so, how quickly?
- Will the connection between economic growth and energy consumption change independently of price changes, because of structural changes in the economic, advancing technology and institutional developments?
- Will prices change (apart from world prices, internal prices may change if there are significant wedges of transport and transformation costs between the internationally traded energy markets and the local consumer market)?

The difficulties of forecasting are well illustrated in Figure 5.7 which shows different forecasts for Chinese energy demand for 2020, made in 1995, compared to a simple mathematical extrapolation of past history.

The 'ZF' forecast originates from the Energy Research Institute of China's State Planning Commission. It assumes that GDP growth continues at 9% to the year 2000 (compared to 9.6% between 1980 and 1993) and then slows to 7.5%, while energy demand grows at about 5% – preserving but not improving the historical relationship between the two. If even higher levels

---

[6] The 1993 ratio from current to PPP is applied to 1985 current data in this calculation.

Figure 5.7 China primary energy consumption

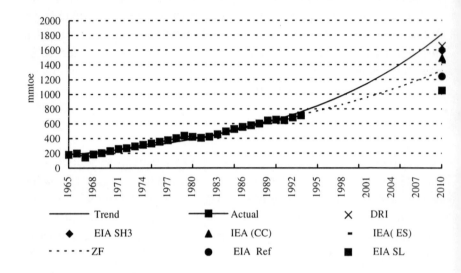

Sources: EIA, IEA, CERI, World Bank.

of GDP per unit of energy are achieved with higher levels of per capita income, this forecast may be overstated.

Fuel choices

Sector mix

Fuel consumption is influenced by sectoral demand. Transportation demands oil. The demand for nuclear power depends on demand for electricity and the load mix in the generating sector. The present mix of fuel in final energy demand in East Asia reflects different stages of industrial development: industrial consumption accounts for roughly two-thirds of final energy demand in China, half in Japan and half in other East Asian countries as a group. The electric power sector consumed 28% of China's primary energy in 1993.[7] For the European Union the corresponding figure is about 30%. The transportation sector was very different, accounting

---
[7] Fengqi (1995).

Figure 5.8 Regional primary energy mix

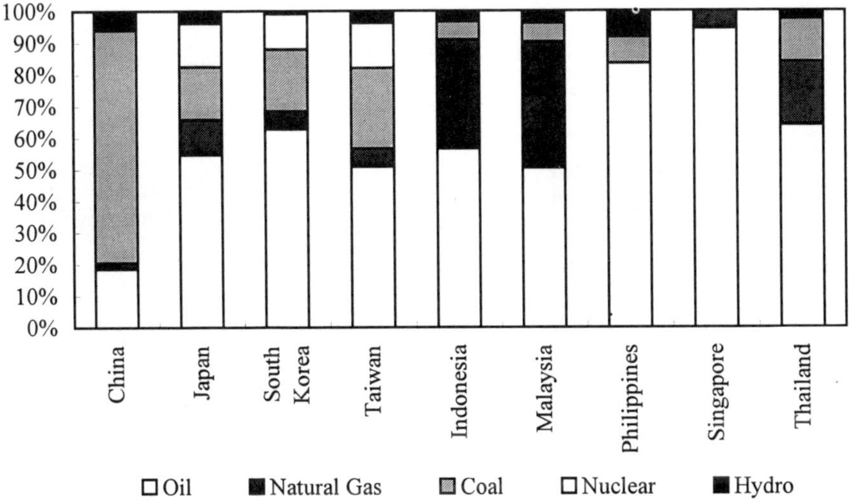

☐ Oil　■ Natural Gas　▨ Coal　☐ Nuclear　■ Hydro

Source: *BP Statistical Review* (1995).

Note: The *BP Statistical Review* figures for hydro-electricity have been converted to oil equivalents on the basis of the equivalent input of fuel to a power station of 33% conversion efficiency, and are thus comparable with the nuclear figures converted on the same basis.

for about 10% of Chinese energy consumption compared to around 25% in the OECD as whole. As the industrial structures in East Asian countries develop, the share of transport in final demand will grow and the share of electricity diminish. This structural change will bring about an improvement in energy use per unit of GDP irrespective of technology, and a steady shift towards transport fuel (oil) and away from electricity generation fuels (in China, coal).

Local supply factors

Each country in East Asia has a different mix of primary energy sources, influenced by the availability and cost of local supply. There are four broad categories which are illustrated in Figure 5.8 for 1994:

• China, the largest energy market in East Asia, over three-quarters of

Figure 5.9 Primary energy fuel mix, %

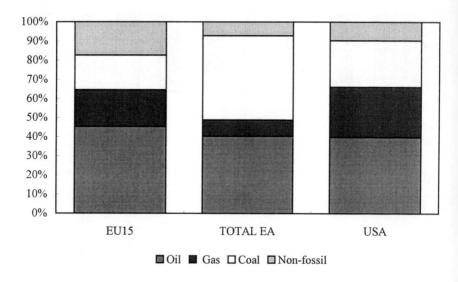

Source: *BP Statistical Review* (1995).

whose energy is supplied by Chinese coal and lignite.[8] China produces and consumes just over a quarter of the world's coal.

- Japan, Taiwan and the Republic of Korea, which have, as a matter of policy, diversified their energy mix by supporting imports of LNG and the construction of nuclear power stations.
- Indonesia and Malaysia, which are exporters of oil and gas (and coal, in the case of Indonesia).
- Countries such as the Philippines, Singapore and Thailand whose consumption is dominated by oil, all or mostly imported.

In aggregate, however, the result is that the energy mix of East Asian countries as a group differs significantly from that of the USA or the EU: East Asia, because of China, is more focused on coal and oil, as Figure 5.9 shows. Nuclear power supplies 15% of primary energy in Japan and

---

[8] For logistical reasons, there is a small trade in coal: exports from the north and imports to the south.

Taiwan, and over 10% in Korea – significantly higher than in the USA (though US nuclear capacity is roughly double that of East Asia).

Energy supply

Because of the variations in the primary energy mix, the issues of importance for energy supply differ between countries. *Coal* is obviously of critical importance to China. The supply questions concern cost, productivity and logistics. There is also a set of forces which may serve to limit the growth in Chinese demand for coal:

- Improved efficiency in power generation.
- A need to reduce pollution in industrial areas – partly by clean-burning technology and scrubbing stack gases, but also by substituting cleaner fuels. This has an international dimension because of the drift of sulphur dioxide emissions across the seas to Korea and Japan and the consequent damage caused by acid rain.
- Finally, in the longer term, a possible Chinese role in the global effort to mitigate the growth in the global emissions of greenhouse gases. The last point – the only one with a truly global geopolitical context – is discussed further in Chapter 7.

Nuclear power plant construction is envisaged in the energy outlooks of Japan, China, Korea (North and South) and Taiwan. The North Korean case has already become a 'geopolitical' issue because of the US interest in minimizing the risk that it perceived in North Korea's plans to proceed on the basis of Russian technology and with independent management of the fuel cycle. These are particular cases of the general question of nuclear developments in developing countries which are discussed further in Chapter 6. They are important in terms of the growth in the world's nuclear business to 2010. The IEA *World Energy Outlook, 1995* 'Energy Savings' case[9] projects an increase in nuclear supply of the order of 350 TWh in East Asia: more than half the 480 TWh net increase projected for world nuclear generation, but only around 2% of world electricity production in

---

[9]   IEA (1995e).

the same projection for 2010. The interesting geopolitical questions about East Asian nuclear expansion arise from international and national geopolitics, not from world energy considerations.

Natural gas and LNG

The outlook for gas supply is complex and uncertain. It depends on the development of large cross-border projects, either for LNG or for pipeline gas, or both. Substantial investment will be required in infrastructure in gas importing countries: to bring gas to industrial and power-generating users in the case of Korea and China, and for reticulated distribution systems for commercial and domestic use in other importing or would-be importing countries. If these investments are made, conditions would exist for rapid increases in demand if supply is available without large increases in price. The challenge is that investment in any one part of the chain from producer to consumer is at risk if investment does not take place in a timely fashion in all parts of the chain. There is no physical logistical network, and no commercial commodity market in which these risks can be managed. Complex, interlocking deals are inevitable. Up to now, these have been developed largely by the major Japanese electricity utilities and trading houses. As more countries become involved, and as the gas market is deregulated in Japan, their influence in the LNG market will be reduced.

The IEA 1995 forecasts seem to imply an increase in gas consumption in East Asia of 80–90 mmtoe, involving an increase in energy market share of around 5%. Most commercial forecasts focus on internationally traded LNG, with estimates of market growth spread around 60–70 mmtoe. Two-thirds of the growth in LNG demand will be outside Japan, including increasing imports to Taiwan and Korea, and possibly new imports to China and Thailand. This will be a reverse of the past situation where more than 80% of the demand has been in Japan.

On the supply side, project scales and timings fluctuate, but roughly one-third of the predicted trade could be provided by existing exporting countries, about the same amount by Qatar, and in the longer term the remainder by some combination of Natuna and Sakhalin supplies.

Beyond that, almost all the new gas will have to come either from longer distances such as Prudhoe Bay in Alaska, or from new exporting areas such as Iran, Oman or Yemen. All these areas are contenders for gas export projects for which there are alternative markets (the USA for Prudhoe Bay, South Asia for Oman and Yemen). There still exists a queue of projects to be managed against expected new demand. The problem will be that the demand will be spread among a number of countries and no longer dominated by Japanese buyers. Developments by, and commitments of, both buyers and developers will be riskier as a result.

Longer-term gas options

In the longer term (probably beyond 2010) there is scope for expanding the natural gas share of the East Asian market substantially through the importation of Russian gas (from Irkutsk and Yakutia) and Turkmen gas by long-distance pipeline. The resources available – though not yet fully proved – might potentially support a further 30–50 mtoe of supply, possibly 3–5% of the total primary energy market in 2010. There are no obvious alternative export markets for these resources. The interdependence of production, transportation, distribution and even consumer investments will be even greater than for LNG. There will be less possibility of switching suppliers or markets, unless or until a much more complex East Asian pipeline system develops.

Importing countries therefore have some choice but also some difficult decisions about commitments. Some of the Russian projects could be advanced relative to, say, Middle East projects or even Indonesian projects in order to diversify sources of supply. Russian pipeline supplies will involve an interdependence of value to exporter and importer and could be robust against political changes as Russian supplies to Europe have been. On the other hand, the financing of such major pipeline projects, with new trading partners, will require serious commitment by governments to guarantee the service of pipeline capital in some way and to some extent. The governments concerned (Russia, China, Korea and possibly Japan) will also have to overcome inhibitions resulting from current diplomatic and political differences – in the Japanese case the border dispute with Russia over the Kurile islands.[10]

Within the framework of intergovernmental agreement or disagreement and security consideration, economics will continue to matter. The traditional competition between a diversity of resource owners each seeking to place their projects in the development queue will continue. The new factor will be competition on the importing side, with China, Korea and possibly Japan seeking long-term cost advantages by securing the commitment of lower-cost supply sources. To the extent that the lower-cost Middle East reserves are committed to Far Eastern projects, they will not be available for commitment to LNG or pipeline export to Europe.

Oil

Supply of oil within the region will continue to grow: China currently produces 36% and Indonesia 19% of the region's oil. Beyond 2000 there may be substantial scope for increasing oil production as advanced technology and economic management techniques are applied ('reserve growth' can happen in China too). There is also significant scope for new discoveries: the region contains part of the Tethyian geology. Half (77 bn bbls) of the region's possible ultimate oil reserves[11] remain to be discovered (in contrast to around 15% in the Middle East). No other region has such a favourable ratio of future discoveries to present remaining oil reserves. Ultimate oil reserves may be more than double those of western Europe. The scope for increasing recovery and 'growth' from existing reserves is dominated by China, with Indonesia and Malaysia as the other key countries.

The reserve endowment suggests that over a twenty-year period, production in the region could meet much of the growing demand, though there are questions of time, access, management and technology. In China, production could increase perhaps 0.5 mmbd by 2000 and 1–2 mmbd by 2010. China would nevertheless become a significant oil importer. The IEA's detailed review of China in its *World Energy Outlook, 1994* suggested imports of 0.9 mmbd by 2000 and up to 2.8

---

[10] These are described fully in Paik (1995).
[11] See Masters (1994).

mmbd by 2010 in the reference case. It is not difficult to generate higher estimates from a combination of high growth in the industrial and transport sectors and low investment in the oil producing sector.

In 'Other East Asia', oil production is likely to increase by 0.5–1 mmbd by 2000 and 1.5–2.5 mmbd by 2010, depending mainly on access to new acreage, the progress of cost-reducing technologies for smaller reservoirs, and the speed of investment in new discoveries. Added production could cover about half the increase in demand of 1.5 mmbd (to 2000) and a third of the increase of 6 mmbd (to 2010) in 'Other East Asia' demand. For the whole region, therefore, imports could grow 1.5–2 mmbd by 2000 and perhaps around 6 mmbd by 2010 – the number could be lower if potential geological prospects are realized. These imports are all likely to come from the Middle East. The relatively low growth in oil demand in Europe and the western hemisphere, combined with the continuing growth in production there (described in Chapter 2), means that increasing dependence by importing countries on Middle East supplies, if it occurs, will be an East Asian rather than a global phenomenon.

A new feature will be a continuing decline in oil exports from Indonesia, as domestic demand absorbs an increasing portion of a static or declining supply. As in other regions, application of new technology and the release of new acreage may postpone or mitigate this trend.

Trade implications

Japan is a major importer of all traded fuels. Some southeast Asian countries are energy exporters.

Imports

The region's energy trade is dominated by Japan. With oil imports flat (the assumed result of policies) the Japanese tenth official Long Term Forecast assumes gas imports increase by 14 mmtoe by 2000, and a further 10 mtoe by 2010, and nuclear capacity increases by 17 mmtoe to 2000 and a further 26 mmtoe by 2010.

LNG and coal are imported by utilities and trading houses. Most non-oil trade takes place under long-term contracts. There is some investment by Japanese trading companies in LNG plant and ships. Japanese National Oil Corporation (JNOC) also supports Japanese companies which invest in exploration for oil.

Chinese imports and exports were insignificant in 1993. Imports began in 1994 and grew in 1995. The trend seems likely to continue. It may be asked whether it will be choked off for economic reasons. In the author's view, this is unlikely: Chinese merchandise exports in 1994 were $116 billion; 1 mmbd of oil imports at $15/bbl would have cost $5.5 billion – six weeks of foreign investment and two weeks of exports at current rates. Chinese exports are forecast to grow at 12% per annum in the next five-year plan.[12] A large, diversified economy with a rapidly expanding manufacturing base and low labour costs has the potential to sustain rapidly rising oil imports.

The region as a whole was only a marginal importer of gas from outside the Pacific (Abu Dhabi). The region as a whole imported oil, though there were exporters in the region (Indonesia, Malaysia, Brunei and Papua New Guinea). As described above, this pattern is expected to change, with China becoming an importer of significant quantities of oil during the next ten years, and the possibility of imports of natural gas increasing in the longer term. The economic significance of energy imports depends on value, rather than volumes. Figure 5.10 shows the position of energy trade in country export and import totals for 1993.

Market structure

Fuel markets in many East Asian countries are being liberalized. In Japan the Petroleum Law expires in 1996; imports of petroleum products were liberalized in 1994. In most Southeast Asian countries (except Indonesia) there are competitive oil markets and foreign as well as domestic competitors.

International short-term and 'spot' trade within the region (and beyond it) is mainly in oil. Singapore is an export refining centre and trading point with an established futures commodity exchange for oil and oil products

---

[12] See *Financial Times*, 6 February 1996.

Figure 5.10 Net energy trade (by value) as % of total exports 1993

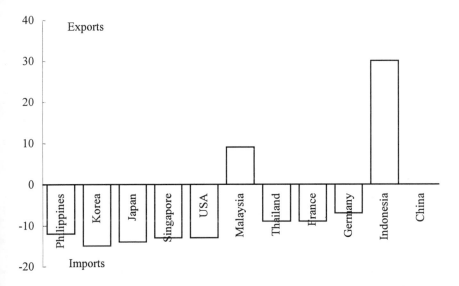

Source: World Bank (1995).

which serves as a pricing point for East Asian short-term oil trading. Independent storage facilities exist in Singapore and are being established in other countries.

By contrast, the international gas trade in the region – almost entirely LNG – is organized under bilateral, long-term contracts between importers (generally Japanese utilities and the Korean Gas Corporation) and exporting producers (generally consortia, which often include Japanese companies as investors). In recent years, changes in supply and demand volumes have generated some spot surplus of LNG, and this trade may develop to the discomfort of the pricing mechanisms for the long-term contracts (which tend to be formula-linked to movements in the oil price and contain considerable inertia).

The growing coal trade – though containing a spot trade which LNG normally does not – is founded on long-term contracts between export mines in Indonesia or Australia and Japanese, Korean or other importing power companies. If pipeline gas supplies develop into Japan and Korea, the potential for interfuel competition (initially through the electricity generating sector) will be enhanced. Since the electricity utilities are buyers of every fuel (including some low-sulphur crude oil for direct burning) and builders of nuclear stations, increasing liberalization and competition in the electricity sector will link the fuel markets more closely together.

The role of governments and energy policies

Energy policy has a priority in most East Asian countries that it has lost in Europe and the USA. There are different reasons for this:

- A sense in Japan of total import dependence on energy imports (other than nuclear).
- A sense in the more rapidly growing countries that expansion of energy supplies is critical to sustaining uninterrupted economic development.
- A stronger state role in the direct management of economic sectors generally than is current in most of Europe and the USA.
- Energy-related environmental concerns which are politically important – urban pollution in most countries, acid rain in China and its downwind neighbours.

The degree and form of government participation in the energy sector vary between countries. Two trends in many countries affect the energy industry as part of wider economic policy changes:

- Liberalization of markets and competition: the Japanese government's 1995 plan for economic deregulation (in sectors including energy) involves, among other things, allowing:
  - the direct import of gasoline outside the refining companies;
  - independent (including foreign) companies to retail gasoline, distribute oil products and refine crude oil;
  - competition between electric utilities, the creation of independent power producers, and competition between gas utilities and electricity utilities.
- Privatization of some state companies and activities (for example power plants in Indonesia). This is not so strong a trend in East Asia as in Latin

America (most East Asian governments have strong national budgets). 'Corporatization' and decentralization in China represent a step which may eventually lead to full privatization.

Japan

The Japanese government appears to be adopting a proactive regional energy strategy, integrated with wider regional political strategies: energy, environmental, and political 'good neighbourliness' objectives combined in programmes to encourage Japanese companies to invest in regional energy supplies and in projects which introduce clean and energy efficient technologies in power plants and major energy-using processes. Japan may reasonably seek a leadership role in regional energy matters, because of its importance and long experience in international energy markets, its long-term participation in extra-regional governmental energy cooperation such as the IEA, and the existence of a long-established mechanism (JNOC) for supporting Japanese investment in foreign oil supplies.

Japanese motivation in such moves is manifold: there is an interest in peaceful and cooperative development in the region, avoiding conflicts; there is an interest in preserving, in a more complex market, the influence which Japan had, through Japanese companies, in selecting the large projects for energy development dedicated to exports to the region (in the past, the LNG and coal projects in Australia and Southeast Asia are examples); there is an interest in providing business opportunities for Japanese firms supplying equipment and undertaking large construction projects; there is an interest in finding profitable investment for Japanese funds. Japan has secured the secretaryship of the APEC committee on energy and it remains to be seen at what pace these activities move beyond statistical and regulatory analysis to policy initiatives: wider considerations than energy are likely to determine energy's role on the agenda.

China

In contrast to the regional tendencies and international experience projected into energy relationships by Japan, China's energy policies are likely to be centred on the two domestic challenges: increasing supply and cleaning up the coal cycle on which the supply will continue to be based for several decades. Clean coal technologies are being adapted and applied. These include coal washing and preparation, briquette coals which contain sulphur absorbers and burn with increased efficiency, coal powder burners with more efficient combustion, fluidized-bed combustion, flue gas treatment, and the use of coal gas-driven turbine generators. There is significant research in coal gasification, oil liquefaction, and coal-water mixture combustion. For China, with a large, diverse and rapidly expanding manufacturing sector, these are indigenous industrial developments in which foreign technology is important, but foreign investment is not necessary except to ensure the efficient and rapid acquisition of the technology. Despite these trends, the Chinese State Planning Commission estimates that Chinese emissions of SO_2 and CO_2 will roughly double between 1990 and 2010.[13] Pollution levels in major Chinese cities are likely to remain distressing for the inhabitants as well as for observers of the global environment.

Indonesia

Indonesian energy policy is also intertwined with other policies, and has regional impact: it is the principal energy exporter within the region (oil, gas and coal). Energy exports are important in the Indonesian economy: oil accounts for around 14% of merchandise exports and gas and coal as much again. The structure of exports is changing: crude oil exports are likely to fall as a result of rising domestic demand and the construction of export refineries (which will add to the diversification of competition in the oil product market in East Asia). Gas exports are likely to grow through a succession of enhancement and new export projects, possibly supported by new gas discoveries. Indonesia has used foreign firms – mainly firms from outside the region – as agents of developments generally on a 50:50 basis. Pressures for liberalization and the opening of the Indonesian economy to more general foreign investment are likely to grow, and Indonesian firms are likely to respond to lower levels of protection at home by seeking a more active role

---

[13] Fengqi (1995).

abroad. This does not seem likely in the primary producing part of the energy industry, but could develop in the refining sector. In short, Indonesia's external energy relations may change as a result of internal economic and structural developments.

Regional institutions

The final characteristic of the East Asia region's energy policy apparatus is the lack of international coordination to address international energy policy issues. Energy has only just become an APEC topic – among many others (see above). ASEAN does not include the major energy countries of Northeast Asia. Only Japan is a member of the IEA, though Korea may join, following its admission to the OECD. Energy projects and environmental issues feature on the agenda of the Asian Development Bank and the Economic Commission for Asia and the Pacific, and get some regional treatment within the regional divisions of the World Bank. Of East Asian countries only Japan has signed the Energy Charter Treaty.

This lack of international institutional structure contrasts with the heavy weight of institutions in Europe such as the European Commission, driven by the single market provisions of the treaties, and in the USA the federal government. Both these regions and Japan are linked in the IEA.

The lack of dedicated energy institutions may be an advantage for East Asia:

'The problem is energy experts above all tend to expect that future development of APEC can centre on energy. In reality, however, energy is just one of the pillars in a line, including such issues as trade, investment and technology transfer.'[14]

East Asian participation in wider energy organizations is unlikely to address its specific energy challenges. The IEA does not embrace non-OECD countries: its 'shared values' have a free-market theme which does not encompass the reality of many East Asian governments' engagement in energy policy. The Energy Charter Treaty might have a role to play but,

---

[14] Ikuta (1995).

like the IEA, it does not envisage governments as promoters of mega-projects – which is what the East Asian situation seems to require.

For companies and governments interested in particular projects, the message is that there is unlikely to be any grand design for East Asian energy. From the precedents of ASEAN and APEC, the more likely development is a loose process of intergovernmental discussions and 'forums' which set a context for specific intergovernmental agreements on specific projects. Negotiating those projects will require attention to the 'context' as well as to the projects. It will be a challenge for outsiders to track and understand the contextual developments, but failure to do so may result in projects being considered 'out of context', with consequent disappointment and frustration for those whose attention is focused narrowly on them.

Conclusions for policy

This simple survey of East Asian energy demand suggests several general implications for policy:

- The region already carries more weight in global energy demand than the EU, and will very soon carry more weight than the USA. Whether and how that weight is translated into international energy markets needs is an important question.
- The expansion of energy supply is critical to sustaining East Asian rates of economic growth. For East Asia, energy security requires continuous investment in new supply, accessible to the countries concerned.
- The mix of primary energy differs between East Asian countries. The existence of local resources explains the domination of coal in China, and of oil and gas in Indonesia and Malaysia. Policies of diversification supported by investment explain the role of LNG and nuclear power in the Republic of Korea and Japan. From the demand side, there appears to be scope for expanding the share of natural gas in these countries' energy markets if the right conditions develop for substantial investments in production, transportation and distribution dedicated to cross-border gas supplies, both from new sources of LNG and from Russian pipeline gas.

- The region as a whole is not very differently placed from the EU and the USA in terms of use of oil: it would be similarly exposed to oil price shocks and to cyclical fluctuations in oil prices. Individual countries within the region are more or less exposed than the region as a whole (as are states within the USA or Europe). But for highly exposed countries in East Asia there is no collective umbrella: no regional strategic petroleum reserve like the SPR in the US, no supply-sharing mechanism like the IEA (except for Japan, which is a member of the IEA; as mentioned above, Korea may join in the near future).

- If global climate change policy is to address the CO_2 emissions which are least productive in terms of GDP – those from coal burning – there is no escape from addressing them in East Asia, and specifically in China (as described below).

- While anti-nuclear policies in Europe and the USA have the effect of constraining the growth of the nuclear construction industry in those countries, the industry will develop in East Asia as the major countries there pursue nuclear expansion to diversify energy supplies.

Key uncertainties

There are some uncertainties which are specific to countries and important enough to have regional and wider implications:

- Will substituting gas exports or diminishing oil exports sustain Indonesia's trade balance in the long term? The Natuna gas project is important in this respect.

- How far, and how fast, will Chinese oil imports grow? They could be constrained, with a cost to economic growth, by balance-of-payments considerations, or security policy. They might be limited by a more expansive policy towards the use of foreign technology and enterprise in the discovery and development of domestic reserves.

Causes of conflict

There are energy policy issues in East Asia which generate locally disturb-ing issues with international implications. One is East Asian countries' rela-tions with the Middle East: energy trading or investment relations with some Middle Eastern countries' (Iran and Iraq, for example) may cut across East Asian countries relations with the USA. Investment in nuclear energy, choice of nuclear plant and fuel supplier may likewise raise issues with the USA and other nuclear countries concerned about nuclear proliferation risks – as in the case of North Korea.

Chinese 'dirty burning' of high-sulphur coal may continue to carry acid rain to damage the ecologies of Korea and Japan. Energy relations are just one part of a complex web of political, economic and historic relations whose management is a continual challenge to policy. Every major coun-try has a menu of conflicts to which energy issues may add and which will constrain solutions based entirely on energy or economic criteria. Projects for pipelines to supply Russian gas to Japan may be closed to Japanese companies as a result of the continuing territorial disagreement over the Kurile Islands. Exploration in the South China Sea may be frustrated because of Chinese claims to economic or territorial sovereignty.[15]

The questions of the reintegration of Taiwan in China, or of the reunifi-cation of Korea, have immense potential to change the balance of power within the region. Sudden and non-consensual steps towards either end could disrupt normal economic relations between countries in the region, and possibly with some countries outside the region.

Reasons for cooperation

Connections also run the other way. Japanese promotion of, and invest-ment in, new energy sources for China, including exploration and devel-opment in China itself, serves both countries' interests: China's in bring-ing additional capital, and Japan's in reducing China's demand for inter-national energy imports for which Japan is a competitor.

Wider political relationships may be assisted by projects for the devel-

---

[15] *Petroleum Economist*, July 1995.

opment of cross-border energy trade and investment. The possibility of developing Russian gas supplies by pipeline to Northeast Asia is the prime example and one which would have implications for world energy markets as well as for the development of economic and business relationships between the countries involved[16] – and perhaps between investors and suppliers from outside the region[17] – for cooperation if energy supplies from outside the region are disrupted.

Within East Asia are some of the most efficient energy economies in the world and some of the least efficient. The differences may be closely connected with different levels of wealth (and thus may narrow as wealth differences narrow). However, improvements may also be achieved through technology and institutional acquisition by the developing from the developed countries within the region. The Japanese government's 'New Earth 21' policy initiative is an example which seeks to promote such technological and institutional progress.

Finally, as global policy for mitigating the emission of greenhouse gases continues to evolve, opportunities may arise for 'joint implementation' in which the OECD signatories of Annex 1 of the UN Framework Convention on Climate Change may bear the cost of introducing technical and institutional improvements which will slow the growth of greenhouse gas emissions by non-OECD East Asian countries.

---

[16] See Paik (1995).

[17] See Stewart (1995).

Chapter 6

Nuclear issues

Peter Beck

Introduction

Beliefs about the future of nuclear energy have changed drastically over the past 20 years – from being seen during the mid-1970s as the main hope of mankind for cheap and abundant energy to today's doubts in many quarters whether it is worth persevering with this energy form in the light of its unresolved problems, dangers, unfavourable economics and unpopularity. This change in perception has been brought about by a number of issues, some global, some more local and national.

To provide an idea of why these changes came about and how they have affected the geopolitical issues relating to this energy form, this chapter first looks at the position of nuclear energy in the mid-1970s and now, before addressing factors specific to nuclear energy, namely radiation and its effect on public attitudes and the connection with nuclear weapons proliferation. This is followed by a glance at how perceptions of the economics of nuclear energy relative to other energy forms and of energy security have changed over the period and what effect the issue of global warming has on these. Finally, before considering the policy issues arising from this analysis, the chapter asks how technological developments might affect the future of nuclear power.[1]

Nuclear energy then and now

The industry in the mid-1970s

The mid-1970s was the period of greatest enthusiasm for nuclear energy. Although at the time world capacity was only some 70 GW_e, the annual rate of growth of capacity was 25% and there were expectations that capacity

---

[1] Most of this chapter is based on Beck (1994), updated where necessary.

would be between 1,500 and 2,000 GW_e by the turn of the century. Even though there was already a strong anti-nuclear lobby in many countries, the promise of a cheap and virtually unlimited source of energy during a period of perceived energy crisis kept most governments and the power generation industry on the side of nuclear enthusiasts. The estimate that 1 kg of uranium can produce as much energy as some 2,000 tonnes of oil was, at the time, a telling argument.

The fuel cycle then envisaged assumed that by reprocessing spent fuel from nuclear reactors and making use of fast breeder reactors (FBRs) which burn plutonium and convert the non-fissile uranium isotope U^{238} into more plutonium, it would eventually be possible to utilize a large proportion, perhaps as much as 80%, of uranium for power production, rather than just the 0.7% of the fissile isotope U^{235} in natural uranium. It was also assumed that FBRs would be in operation well before the end of the century, so starting the move into the 'plutonium economy', when plutonium would become the main fuel for nuclear reactors.

The key issues at that time were concerns that there could be a shortage of uranium unless FBRs were phased in quickly, and questions of how best to deal with the increasingly vociferous public opposition to nuclear power.

The industry today

Nuclear energy currently supplies some 7% of the world's primary commercial energy and about 17% of electric power; some 430 reactors are in operation in 30 countries with a total capacity of about $350GW_e$ of which 70% is in OECD countries.[2] Around 60 reactors are under construction, although some of these may never be completed, and compared to the estimates of twenty years ago capacity at the end of the century may not quite reach $400GW_e$. Nearly 80% of reactors are light water reactors (LWRs), originally developed in the 1950s by the US Navy for propelling nuclear submarines.

The nuclear fuel cycle, as utilized today, is shown diagrammatically in

---

2 See Table 6.2 for a regional breakdown of capacity.

Figure 6.1 Nuclear fuel cycle

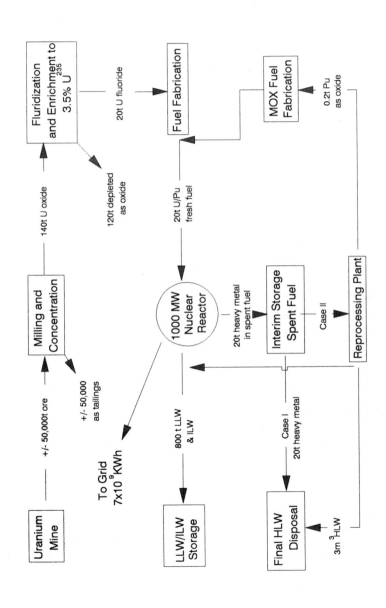

Source: Author.

Figure 6.1. Fission of the isotope of uranium, U^{235}, is the basic source of heat in the reactors. As already mentioned, its content in natural uranium is only 0.7%, most of the rest being the non-fissile U^{238}. The uranium has therefore to be enriched to a U^{235} content of about 3.5% before use as fuel in the form of uranium oxide. In the reactor much of the U^{235} is destroyed and some of the U^{238} is converted into the fissile element plutonium, which on fission adds to the heat generation in the reactor. As fission products, some of which poison the reaction, build up, the fuel has to be removed; in addition to U^{238} and highly radioactive fission products, such spent fuel contains some unconverted U^{235} and between 0.5 and 1% of plutonium.

Two means of dealing with this spent fuel are employed at present. In Case I, the material would be considered as high-level nuclear waste and disposed of in irretrievable deep underground storage after some years in interim storage to reduce radioactivity. In Case II, the spent fuel is reprocessed to separate out the unconverted fraction of uranium, the plutonium and the radioactive reaction products. The uranium can be recycled to the enrichment plant, the reaction products are taken to final storage, and the plutonium can be mixed with natural uranium to form fresh reactor fuel (called mixed oxide fuel, MOX). Although Case II makes better use of natural uranium, a number of countries and especially the USA prefer the once-through Case I and argue against the need to reprocess spent fuel.

As will be seen below, the industry has not been able to allay public unease about nuclear power, an attitude which has become stronger and more 'respectable' during the past twenty years; nor has it been able to deliver the expected economic advantages. As a result, it has lost the support of a number of governments and of large sectors of the power industry, especially where privately owned and operating under competitive conditions. Nevertheless, the nuclear industry itself continued to believe in its long-term future, and although it now accepts that there is ample uranium to fuel the far smaller industry of today, the fuel cycle assumed in the 1970s, including reprocessing and use of FBRs, is still much of the industry's longer-term aim.

Safety, radiation and public attitudes
The 1970s

The possibility of releasing radioactivity into the environment became an early public concern. In addition to fears about catastrophic release, say by a reactor meltdown, there were worries about leaks from all types of nuclear plants and from nuclear waste dumps. The original civil programme in the USA went to great lengths to reassure the public about the safety of reactor designs, but the industry's assurances were rather dented by incidents in the military programmes of the nuclear weapons states, which, though kept secret, slowly leaked out, and by events during the 1970s which showed *inter alia* that nuclear regulators in the USA were at times overruled when criticizing reactor designs. These incidents, plus a general fear of radiation and its effects, caused public opinion to become risk-averse about nuclear power. This increased local resistance to siting nuclear facilities or dumps and, at least in democratic countries, caused severe delays in obtaining planning permission for new plants. The industry and governments attempted to show that this mistrust was misplaced by increasing safety provisions and by attempting to define safe limits of radiation doses; but to little avail. Individual attitudes, which are the basis of public attitudes, appear to be formed by aggregating, perhaps subconsciously, a number of beliefs about risks and benefits; complex statistical arguments and comparisons employed by the industry played little part in such an analysis which on the whole found nuclear energy too risky for the perceived benefits. When it came to believing governments and the industry or the environmental lobbies, the public in many countries chose the latter.

Attitudes today

Since the 1970s there have been many incidents and developments to affect today's attitudes.

Reactor safety In 1979 a reactor at the Three Mile Island nuclear plant in the USA suffered from a near-meltdown, an accident the nuclear industry had long maintained could not possibly happen. Although the accident caused no injuries or significant escape of radioactivity, it reinforced public disquiet about nuclear safety in the USA. Then, in 1986 came Chernobyl. Although it was accepted that this accident was the result of bizarre operating errors and that the standard of design of the reactor involved was far below that acceptable outside the Communist bloc, its terrible effect on the surrounding area and the wide radioactive contamination as far as Lapland and the UK greatly strengthened the anti-nuclear lobby's position that nuclear power is too dangerous and should be phased out as soon as possible. The event also showed that nuclear safety is not just a local matter; it is a geopolitical issue. A serious incident anywhere can have a direct effect on many countries and affect the future of the nuclear industry throughout the world.

Another lesson learnt was the lack of international assistance in tackling the many problems which arose from the Chernobyl accident. There appeared to be plenty of international interest and willingness to give advice, but far less willingness to provide practical help with funds and equipment. There was pressure from the West to close all reactors using the Chernobyl design, but little interest in finding practical ways of achieving this without causing massive shortages of power, and in finding funds to replace such nuclear capacity. In the event, Russia has managed to improve the operational safety of these types of reactors and does not accept the need for phasing them out early, but that view is not accepted everywhere.

All this shows that there is, at present, no international system which certifies the safety and security of nuclear installations and which can initiate action should it find facilities below minimum acceptable standards. Nuclear safety, however international in effect, is still seen to be of national concern only.

Since the Three Mile Island accident much thought has been given to making nuclear reactors safer and it is presently said that today's reactor designs have a chance of a serious failure of only one in a million reactor operating years. That, however, assumes official US standards of construction, maintenance and operation, which cannot always be guaranteed everywhere (even in the USA) for the full life of a plant. Furthermore, should nuclear energy expand, during the next half-century, to become a major energy resource, there could be well over 1,000 reactors in perhaps

50 countries by 2050. Doubts have been expressed whether the present designs are sufficiently safe for such an expansion, and the need to reduce the chance of failure by at least a further factor of ten has been suggested.

This is another area of strong disagreement between the industry and its critics, which on this subject include influential past members of the industry, claiming that the present LWR designs can never be made sufficiently safe to become generally acceptable.

The back-end of the fuel cycle The first commercial large-scale reprocessing plants for the civil industry came on-stream during the present decade. Here again, design standards have been much tightened, but the current process is complex and unless very firm operating and maintenance control is maintained at all times, periodic accidental discharge of some radioactive streams cannot be ruled out. Operators maintain that the chance of a significant discharge is minimal, but opponents disagree, with the public tending to believe the opponents more than the industry. The concerns expressed by the Irish government about the risk of the reprocessing plant on the west coast of England contaminating the Irish Sea illustrate the sensitivity of the issue. Even if the present operators are fully justified in their stance, here again the question has to be asked whether the present process is safe enough for major expansion of nuclear energy via plutonium recycling, when there could be 20 to 30 such plants scattered throughout the world. Acceptability of reprocessing in general has also been hit by the stance of the US government that in the civil domain of nuclear energy it is unnecessary and brings with it safety and security risks.

One factor feeding public mistrust is the fact that there are at present no global mandatory and monitoring systems in place to ensure that new designs of nuclear plants, storage facilities and means of transportation are safe and that operating and maintenance standards of all such facilities are of the required high level at all times. There is, therefore, the danger that short cuts to reduce cost could be taken, or that discipline could become lax, which might eventually lead to another Chernobyl. Accidents in other industries which pride themselves on having very high standards show such fears to be well justified; Piper Alpha in oil, Bhopal and Sevesso in chemicals spring to mind.

The fact that radioactive clouds do not respect national frontiers has further increased public fears because feeling safe has become not just a matter of trusting one's own government and industry, but also that of one's neighbours. If one country believes that another has unsafe facilities but that it is refusing to deal with the problem, serious conflicts can be foreseen.

With all these problems and disagreements in mind, it is not surprising that the past twenty years appear to have done little to assure the public that nuclear energy is acceptably safe and environmentally benign. With few exceptions, the anti-nuclear lobbies are alive and strong in most countries where dissent is tolerated.

Weapons connection – proliferation
Background

The issue of weapons proliferation and the spread of the peaceful use of nuclear energy revolves around the question of how far involvement in the latter could assist a country or an organization to acquire sufficient fissile materials for one or more nuclear weapons. Atomic weapons use U^{235} or plutonium as the explosive. The purity of these materials has to be sufficient to achieve a dense enough mass (the critical mass) in which conditions for the explosion can occur. For uranium the critical mass is around 25 kg. It also requires an enrichment to 90%+ U^{235}, i.e. far higher than for use in power reactors. For plutonium, weapons-grade material, produced in special reactors, contains a preponderance of Pu^{239} and has a critical mass of below 10 kg. However, plutonium derived from normal civil power production can be used in a weapon even though it has a greater mix of other Pu isotopes; it is more difficult to use and requires a critical mass of more than 10 kg.

Because uranium enrichment to weapons-grade quality was seen to be a very difficult step, availability of reactor fuel containing enriched uranium is not regarded as a major threat to cause proliferation. The situation with plutonium is different; its availability in a pure form from reprocessing units or even when contained in fresh MOX fuel, from which it could easily be removed by relatively simple chemical processing, could make it easier for countries or terrorists to acquire nuclear weapons capability.

Concern about proliferation has caused tension and disagreements about the spread of nuclear energy ever since 1945, with sometimes one view and sometimes the other gaining the upper hand. Already in the 1940s a bill was introduced by Senator McMahon to the US Congress, proposing to restrict use of atomic energy to US defence and retain all secrets within the USA. Although the start of the Cold War pushed US policy towards such a strategy, President Eisenhower's 'Atoms for Peace' programme during the 1950s promised US cooperation for the global development of the peaceful use of atomic power. That involved the setting up of the International Atomic Energy Agency (IAEA) with the dual remit of promoting nuclear energy worldwide and preventing the spread of nuclear weapons. In 1968, there followed the UN Nuclear Non-Proliferation Treaty (NPT), renegotiated in 1995 and extended indefinitely as a result. The IAEA was given the responsibility for keeping safeguards up to date and monitoring adherence to the NPT by its signatories, which by now include 178 of the 182 member nations of the UN.

During the height of the Cold War concerns about proliferation became less important than the threat of nuclear war between East and West, and lobbies concentrated on nuclear disarmament rather than on proliferation. The issue had only a small effect on the rapid build-up of interest in civil nuclear power during the 1960s and 1970s, especially after the oil 'crisis' of 1973/4.

Since that time, however, perceptions have changed. The then expectation of a rapid move into the 'plutonium economy' brought the issue of proliferation to the fore again. Fears grew, especially in the USA, about the relationship between increasing the spread of nuclear power plus moving to plutonium recycle, and increasing the risk of proliferation. During this period most of the enriched uranium for power production outside the Communist bloc came from the USA and political forces felt that more control over the destination and use made of this material should be exerted. This pressure culminated in the Nuclear Non-Proliferation Act (NNPA) of 1978 which required foreign governments to obtain 'prior consent' from the USA before activities such as export or reprocessing could be undertaken with nuclear materials based, or even partly based, on US-exported enriched uranium. At the same time, US official policy turned against the major use of plutonium and decided to forgo reprocessing of spent reactor fuel within its civil nuclear programme; a few years later it also stopped work on the prototype FBR programme. It thus effectively abandoned the concept of the 'plutonium economy', at least for the foreseeable future.

As a result of these moves, other countries started having doubts about being able to rely on the USA for fuel for their civil nuclear facilities and became determined to make other arrangements for enrichment and reprocessing capacity. They also carried on with the development of FBRs, still believing that plutonium recycle was an essential part of their longer-term energy policy. For this reason, they started experimenting with reprocessing and some placed contracts for reprocessing spent fuel with the UK and France, enabling both to install large-scale reprocessing facilities. Today, some 19 states have successfully built and operated reprocessing facilities, though most of them on a small pilot scale only.[3] Despite this disagreement between the USA and other countries, and other difficulties surrounding the NPT regime, proliferation does seem to have been constrained, and even though this may largely have been due to the good sense of countries, there is little doubt that the international regime had helped. Beyond the five official 'nuclear weapons states' (China, France, UK, USA and Soviet Union), moves to acquire nuclear weapons largely took place as a result of regional friction in the Middle East and the Indian subcontinent. Most of the countries involved in these activities were not signatories to the NPT and were, therefore, not under IAEA inspection.

The situation today

Worries about proliferation have increased considerably during the last few years, the main reasons being:

Doubts about the effectiveness of IAEA surveillance Recent experience with Iraq showed that even a country that is party to the NPT and under surveillance by the IAEA can still go ahead with the clandestine development of nuclear weapons capability. Similarly, North Korea, also party to the NPT,

---

[3]   Glen Seaborg *et al.* (1995), footnote 10.

decided on actions in 1992/3 which showed that if a country wishes to develop such capability, there is little the world community can do. In this case, only very strong political pressure by the USA (hopefully) persuaded North Korea to change its plans. The NPT regime can make it harder for a country to acquire nuclear weapons, but it cannot stop it, especially as there are always 'rogue' organizations, even within major OECD countries, which, for a requisite reward, are willing to provide illegitimate help.

The threat of terrorism While previously the main proliferation threat was seen to come from states with nuclear weapons ambition, to this has now been added greater public awareness of the terrorist threat, whereby, with or without connivance by a state, nuclear material might be seized by clandestine organizations and forged into a weapon that however crude and unreliable, could become a potent threat in the hands of terrorists. Weapons-grade uranium and plutonium would be the ideal material for such groups, but reactor-grade plutonium would also suit their purpose.

Delay to the availability of final disposal facilities for nuclear waste Spent fuel contains highly radioactive contaminants which makes it more difficult and dangerous to handle, so in a sense safeguarding the contained plutonium against easy separation. It is, therefore, not a suitable material for terrorists, although countries with access to reprocessing techniques and not too worried about the survival of the workforce might be able to make use of it. However, after some decades, much of this radioactivity has decayed, so making the plutonium in spent fuel more readily accessible.

It has now become clear that the plans of the 1970s for the final disposal of spent fuel and high-level waste by deep burial are in trouble. Although initially it was thought that the first deep storage would be ready by the mid-1980s, it is now doubtful whether any will be operational before 2015–20. More detailed examination of possible sites has shown a number of uncertainties and it is even said that the whole concept of guaranteed safe irretrievable permanent isolation may have to be rethought. If, as is quite likely, irretrievability cannot be guaranteed, deep geological storage could become the plutonium mine of future generations.[4]

---

[4] Bowman, 'Weapons and Commercial Plutonium Ultimate Disposition Choices', ch. 17 in Garwin *et al.* (1994.)

Table 6.1 World nuclear capacity and cumulative spent fuel production regional breakdown, 1995

Region	Nuclear capacity, (GWe)	Cumulative spent fuel production	
		000 t	Fissile Plutonium content t
North America	120	63	305
Western Europe	122	80	305
Eastern Europe & CIS	45	21	85
Far East	55	17	100
Other	6	5	15
Total world	348	186	810
So far reprocessed		23	100
Spent fuel in store		163	710

Source: E. Rodwell *et al.* (1996), Table D1.

Meanwhile, spent fuel continues to be kept in temporary storage, mostly on nuclear generating sites. Currently, there may be some 160,000 tonnes of spent fuel, containing about 700 tonnes of plutonium, stored in such facilities in 29 countries (See Table 6.1). In addition, around 25,000 tonnes have been reprocessed, providing some 100 tonnes of plutonium, most of which is also in temporary storage. Some of the spent fuel storage will run out of space within the next ten years, and urgent action is needed to ensure that the ever-increasing amount of this material will be securely stored and not cause risks of proliferation. There are IAEA standards for such storage, but except for members of Euratom, there is no international monitoring to ensure that these standards are adhered to.

Break-up of the Soviet Union The break-up of the Soviet Union saw the end of the East–West nuclear confrontation. The successor states are going through gigantic changes which, at least in the short term, imply reduced levels of law and order and a great lack of funds. There are therefore concerns whether the nuclear weapons under past Soviet control will continue to be adequately safeguarded, especially against theft.

Nuclear disarmament Perversely, the dangers of proliferation have been underlined by the partial nuclear disarmament resulting from the START treaties. These require dismantling of nuclear weapons by the USA and Russia, which is taking place over a period of some 15 years and should provide around 200 tonnes of weapons–grade plutonium plus 1,200 tonnes of weapons-grade uranium which will no longer be part of the military stockpile. The uranium can be 'denatured' by blending it with uranium residues from enrichment plants, so making it suitable for reactor fuel and no longer of use in weapons, whereupon it can be stored in that form until used by power stations. No such option is available for the plutonium. Whether the material is used in MOX fuel, or disposed of by deep burial, or by a number of other means under study in the USA and Russia, all the alternatives will take considerable time to come to fruition and meanwhile such weapons-grade plutonium has to be seen as the ideal material for proliferators. With only 5–10 kg needed for a bomb, can such material be sufficiently closely protected to eliminate the risk of such a small quantity being smuggled out?

All these factors mean that proliferation dangers have now gained far more political attention than some twenty years ago. This raises some difficult issues both about short-term policies, such as the need for secure storage for the increasing stocks of plutonium and spent fuel, and long-term issues, e.g. whether large-scale recycle of plutonium involving many countries, such as envisaged in the 'plutonium economy', can ever be made sufficiently secure. That, in turn, throws doubts on the future of a fuel cycle which includes FBRs and reprocessing of spent fuel, the cycle still preferred by much of the world's nuclear industry.

Economics and energy security
Economics of nuclear power – changed perspectives
Much of the original impetus for nuclear power in the USA and, later,

world-wide came from the assumption that this source of power would be very competitive with oil and coal. By the mid-1970s it became clear that these initial promises might not be fulfilled: far higher capital cost than originally estimated, longer building times, increased complexity and difficulties in start up of nuclear stations quickly reduced the power industry's enthusiasm for nuclear energy. Bearing in mind the strict regulatory system for the US power industry and the increasing unpopularity of nuclear power during the 1970s, it is not surprising that the rapid expansion of nuclear power in the USA came to an abrupt halt, with no new orders for plant since 1978.

However, with the then prevailing belief that oil prices would rise sharply for the rest of the century, possibly reaching $50–60 per barrel, the longer-term economics of nuclear power still looked satisfactory and the nuclear industry and many governments presumed that rapid world-wide expansion would continue with full plutonium recycle and FBRs in operation well before the year 2000. Many of the decisions made towards the end of the 1970s, such as the French and UK reprocessing deals with other countries, were based on these assumptions. The period since then has, however, turned out quite differently:

Competition from oil and natural gas   The 1980s saw oil prices falling and far greater optimism about the longer-term availability and price stability of oil and natural gas. That further increased the economic disadvantage of nuclear energy. With the advent of gas-fired combined cycle power plants, there is, for the present, little doubt that natural gas is now the most economic fuel for power production. As seen in Table 6.2, capital cost per kW(e) is about a quarter of that of nuclear power, and time from decision to start-up of plant is much reduced, perhaps by two-thirds.

Unspecified liabilities   Nuclear power has some additional costs which are so far ill defined. There is no agreement on how to deal with spent fuel and thus about the cost of its eventual disposal, nor are there reliable estimates for the cost of high-level waste storage, or about the provisions necessary for dismantling and decontaminating redundant plant. There is also the

Table 6.2 Capital costs and project time for generating plant

	Gas	Coal	Nuclear
Capital cost, $/kW	500–700	900–1,300	2,000+
Project time, years			
Pre-construction	1	1–2	2
Construction	2	4–5	6–7
Total	3	5–7	8–9

Source: Beck (1994), Table 5.1.

issue of insurance against catastrophic accidents, such as Chernobyl. In the past, governments tended to take the responsibility for such factors, but in some countries they are now attempting to disengage from this responsibility and leave it to the private sector. That, plus the public distrust of nuclear energy, offers a bleak picture for early expansion of nuclear energy, at least for those countries where decisions are left to the market place.

Global warming The one positive factor for the future of nuclear energy which has come to the fore since the early 1980s is the issue of global warming. As evidence accumulates that the world may have to limit CO_2 emission and therefore the use of fossil fuels, the fact that nuclear power does not emit CO_2 has given the industry new hope for an expanding future. The only other energy sources with that advantage are some of the renewable energy forms, but there is doubt whether these alone would be sufficient to combat global warming.

The nuclear industry is attempting to make use of this advantage by arguing that it does not face a level playing field because it has to carry the costs of cleaning up the environment, while fossil fuels do not; as an example, should 'owing to its effect on global warming' discharge of CO_2 carry a large penalty, the economics of nuclear power could be transformed. However, whether correct or not, decisions about such penalties lie with governments, and as they have to consider the competitiveness of their economies, wider international agreements (perhaps on the lines of the Montreal protocol about saving the ozone layer) may well be necessary before such action becomes a realistic possibility.

It will be seen that from today's view of the comparative economics between nuclear energy and fossil fuels, there is no incentive to install new nuclear capacity. This, however, does not imply that no more nuclear reactors will be built until this perception has changed.

Energy security Notwithstanding the disappointing economics of nuclear power, countries such as France and Japan, which have few indigenous energy resources, continued to favour this energy form. Reinforced by the oil crises of the 1970s and the expectation that sooner or later the price of oil and gas will rise, or that global warming will limit the use of fossil fuels, they took the strategic decision that the expansion of nuclear power would give them far greater energy security than dependence on oil and gas imports.

Favouring nuclear energy for strategic reasons appears to be spreading to a number of East Asian countries whose economies need rapid expansion of electric power. Their interest in nuclear power seems to indicate that in an uncertain world they are willing to pay a premium for reducing dependence of their economies on imported fuel.[5] Yet other countries which are rich in energy resources are also showing an interest in expanding nuclear power. This may stem from having to take into account vast transportation problems to move local fuels to where they are needed (China); or it may be felt that local oil or gas resources are better used to bring in foreign exchange (Russia, Indonesia). Because of the high capital cost, but low fuel cost, of nuclear power, there could also be situations where developing countries feel that it could be easier to obtain funds for capital investment than for ongoing imports of fuel.

It can be seen that there is no 'correct' answer to whether or not a country utilizes nuclear power. If a government believes that for strategic reasons it wishes to back this power, it can construct the playing-field accordingly. Should a government decide that it has no strategic reasons to inter-

---

[5] Ryukichi Imai (1995).

fere in the choice by the market of fuels for power production, nuclear power has, at present, little chance of being chosen. Unless another energy crisis changes perception again, many problems and public distrust will have to be resolved before the fortunes of nuclear energy in most OECD countries can revive. If, however, economic growth continues in a number of developing countries, we could see a surprising increase in the expansion of the world's nuclear industry.

Alternatives to today's technology

At the end of the 1970s the nuclear industry appeared confident that the fuel cycle leading to the 'plutonium economy' and the technology used in the various processes would carry the industry forward to become a major world energy resource. That there were problems in the areas of security, safety, economics and public attitudes was accepted, but it was felt that steady development of the existing technology plus a PR effort to 'sell' the advantages of nuclear power would resolve these. Since that time, doubts have been thrown on these beliefs, and alternatives to today's technology have been looked at, largely in two areas.

Safety of power reactors

The present workhorse of the nuclear industry is the LWR (see Figure 6.1). The scale-up required to make it economically usable for commercial power generation indicated the need for more safety features and these were added as designs for second and third generation plants were developed. They were all 'engineered safety' provisions, i.e., as safety problems were identified, changes to the design, controls or operating procedure were made to overcome them. Critics, however, can always ask whether there may be safety problems which have not been identified and it is impossible to demonstrate that there have been no such omissions. As a result and whether right or wrong, public distrust seems likely to continue. If, as has been mentioned, there is the need for even greater security against major accidents, there are increasing doubts whether hanging still more safety measures onto a new design would not be counter-productive.

Because of these difficulties, work in a number of countries was devoted to developing an 'inherently safe' reactor, which in a emergency would, by making use of the laws of physics, shut itself down without needing human assistance or the operation of mechanical equipment such as valves or pumps. A number of designs have been tested on a laboratory scale, but the work has not yet reached the stage of building demonstration units. Sufficient has, however, been done to be able to state that in principle it is possible to produce a design where safety should be sufficiently transparent to be understandable by the sceptical expert and therefore perhaps acceptable to the sceptical public.

The fuel cycle

Here there are a number of problems:

- Doubts have been expressed whether the cycle chosen during the 1970s – recycle of plutonium, via reprocessing and FBRs – is sufficiently proliferation-proof.
- The chosen design for FBRs has been found to be difficult to scale up for commercial use and is very costly. After some 40 years of trying, no viable design is so far available.
- If the once-through fuel cycle is chosen with no reprocessing, there may not be sufficient uranium available to sustain major expansion of nuclear energy beyond the middle of the next century.
- The process used for reprocessing spent fuel was developed 50 years ago to produce weapons-grade materials. It is complex and makes large quantities of nuclear waste.
- Some of the nuclear waste produced from this cycle remains dangerous for tens of thousands of years. That has made final disposal not just a difficult technical and economic matter but also a political and moral one.

Work to overcome, or reduce, these problems has shown possible ways of achieving this aim. The key is the use of Fast Neutron Reactors (FNRs), akin to the FBRs, but for destroying plutonium and other long-lived radioactive elements rather than breeding plutonium from uranium, which is the purpose of the FBR. At least on a small scale, such FNRs seem more stable and easier to run than FBRs and their use could reduce, or even eliminate, long-lived nuclear waste. Secure storage for 300 years, rather than 10^{4-5} years, is being talked about.

Different reprocessing steps are also being looked at, including some for which it is claimed that plutonium and other fission products could be recycled without leaving the nuclear reactor site, so reducing the possibility of proliferation. Laboratories in Russia, France, the USA, Canada and Japan are working on these schemes. Again, none of them is beyond the pilot stage.

It can be seen that recent advances in technology have shown signs that some of the more intractable problems besetting the future of nuclear energy might be overcome, thereby making this energy form safer and perhaps more acceptable. Unfortunately, the step from a concept which appears sound from laboratory work to a process which is ready to be used commercially is long and expensive.

The development dilemma

From bitter experience, utilities are wary of using new and untried technology. Before new designs can reach the position of being of interest to them, new processes will have to go through the stages of detailed design, then experience with a semi-scale and finally a commercial-scale prototype. Such a programme would take at least a decade or two and large funds. Much time and money is therefore needed before it will be possible to judge whether the above concepts truly provide the answers. But can such an effort be mounted under today's conditions, and if so, by whom and how would the work be funded?

There are several problems to be considered. To decide whether a major new process, say a new type of reactor, has any chance of becoming a commercial success, may take some tens of millions of dollars. To bring it to commercial availability might take $2-4 billion and fifteen to twenty years. Usually, a number of laboratories throughout the world work on similar projects and arrive at different solutions. Each will be confident and have good technical reasons to believe that its solution is best. Not all schemes can be chosen, even for the first hurdle, but who chooses? Choice for the second step is much harder because of the scale of the commitment.

There is never a guarantee that a process will be a success, even if it meets all technical specifications. Other developers may have got there first, or there may no longer be the need for the process. However effective the development, the risks are very high, especially now that there is global competition. In the past, many of these high risks were funded by defence, where there is not such a close connection between success and monetary success. That goes for nuclear energy especially, and it is often said that the reason the LWR became the most widely used reactor was the fact that it was developed for the US Navy with no expense spared. With defence expenditure now under pressure and far more closely targeted, that is no longer a realistic option.

Until some ten years ago, there was general acceptance that such development risks have to be taken by governments, as they involved the longer-term interests of their country. Now, because of financial pressures on governments and bad experience with some government-funded schemes, there is pressure for them to withdraw from such sponsorship and leave it to private companies, which should have a better feel for what the market is likely to need. Unfortunately, when it comes to projects with lead times as long as one or two decades, there are few reliable market signals to guide such decisions. So with no guarantee of success at the end, the risk is too great for private companies to take on such a task. For the present, therefore, there is a void.

Although this void affects all energy forms where there are needs for new processes which will take decades to commercialize, the effect on nuclear power may be more severe than on other energy forms because of its capital-intensive nature. Until this issue is resolved, the world is stuck with today's technology.

The geopolitical issues identified

The above analyses lead to a number of issues with a geopolitical dimension. As will be seen, some are related to safety and security and require early action, while others, although more long-term, need more international debate before specific actions can be taken. Most, however, cannot readily be left to the 'market', but require political judgment of governments.

The future of nuclear energy

For the present, countries' views about the future of nuclear energy are severely split. Many, especially in OECD countries, like to leave the choice of primary energy to the 'market place' and with unfavourable economics, safety and security risks and public unpopularity, the choice of nuclear energy rather than fossil fuel is unlikely, even for replacement capacity. A number of countries in the developing world, on the other hand, wish to follow the example of countries such as France and Japan, and make nuclear power a major part of their generating strategy. As these countries include the fast-growing East Asian bloc, some South American countries and India, all requiring vast expansion of their generating capacity, it may well be that the future growth of nuclear energy is slipping from the control of the OECD countries (which now have some 70% of total nuclear capacity), and especially of the USA.

So far, the USA has had sufficient technological, economic and political clout to make its voice heard in the nuclear energy field. However, its present internal policies – rejection of reprocessing, strong cut-back of R&D expenditure, and leaving utilities to choose whatever primary energy they wish (which is likely to lead to a slow run-down of the US nuclear capacity) – are slowly weakening its influence. That is especially so, as a number of countries, such as Russia with its large and ambitious nuclear industry and an excess of well-experienced scientists and engineers, have the technological experience not to need US know-how or equipment.

The question is, therefore, whether the USA will be able – or will wish – to continue to police the industry, as it has done with North Korea and as it is currently trying to do with Iran. Then, a further question is whether such policing will continue to be necessary, and if so, how it might be made sufficiently powerful to have an effect.

Safety and security

If the present view about the risks associated with this energy form are accepted, then an expansion into many new countries would make the situation more dangerous. That is not a matter of questioning whether countries are capable of building and operating nuclear facilities safely and securely, but simply a matter of statistics and logic that more new sites, wherever these are, increase the overall risk. It is, therefore, necessary to take steps which would reduce the risk of major accidents and of proliferation.

Accepting that over a period of at least two or three decades, little help can be expected from the development of new nuclear processes, the appropriate area for such steps is in ensuring that all installations are safe and secure. This means that a regime is needed which would check and monitor the standards of design, construction and operation of reactors and all other nuclear facilities, including storage and transport in the civil domain. Such an organization would give confidence to the world that facilities accepted by it are at or above the minimum standard specified by a body such as the IAEA, and that any reduction in standards will be brought into the open. There are already voluntary organizations to provide help and guidance when requested, such as the World Association of Nuclear Operators, but such bodies cannot act unless asked, have no remit to monitor, and do not have the facilities to provide assistance in terms of funds or equipment.

Such a regime will be difficult to set up; governments and industry tend to be suspicious of ever more international 'interference', but there can be ways of tackling such problems which could be more acceptable. However it were organized, progress can only be made if the major nuclear states, and especially the USA, agree to make use of such services and are therefore in a position to put pressure on others. Although such a regime could not stop deliberate evasion of standards, it would be able to cope with the more likely incidents of organizations trying to cut too many corners or becoming blasé about their operating or maintenance standards.

Proliferation and the balance of terror

When it comes to the link between the civil use of nuclear energy and pro-liferation, plutonium in spent fuel or imported MOX fuel has a pivotal role. The suspicion by a country that an unfriendly neighbour may be aiming at acquiring nuclear capability, and that therefore it must do likewise so as to establish a balance of terror, can easily cause both to work towards achiev-ing that aim. It is said that this was the case between India and Pakistan; nei-ther is a signatory to the NPT and therefore their facilities are not subject to international inspection. It had been hoped that IAEA inspection under the NPT would reduce such suspicion, but, unfortunately, the case of Iraq has now shown that a state can hide its activities from IAEA inspection and not comply with the terms of the treaty by using undeclared nuclear facilities.

Unless this is dealt with, there is bound to be more and more suspicion between countries as more acquire nuclear reactors. To reduce this risk, it may be necessary to make it a standard requirement that a country is only given clearance to import nuclear plant and fuel if it accepts that the IAEA has unlimited access in the country to ensure that no undeclared facilities exist (full-scope safeguards). Whatever the mechanism, it seems essential to find some internationally accepted means of tying up the expansion of nuclear facilities with acceptance by the relevant countries of enhanced safeguard requirements under the NPT.

Nuclear power and global warming

Were nuclear power generally acceptable, the issue of global warming and therefore the possibility of having to limit use of fossil fuels would give this energy form a great boost. Unfortunately, in reality there appears to be little dialogue between the nuclear industry and its proponents and those concerned with global warming. The latter therefore look towards other means of reducing fossil fuel use, such as increasing the efficiency of ener-gy use and developing the many forms of renewable energy. Yet, at present there is no certainty that renewable energy plus efficiency will be suffi-cient to curb global warming, especially in the light of the highly uncertain future energy demand of the developing world. Uncertainties today are such that we should not readily forgo the option of having the ability of making major use of nuclear energy sometime in the next century, but the question has then to be asked whether, bearing in mind the safety, security and acceptability problems, major expansion based on today's technology will ever be a realistic option.

Such doubts, however, must not imply that the debate on global warming issues can ignore the effect of nuclear energy, both as it is today and as it might develop in the future.

The development predicament

Laboratories are at present working on a number of developments which could resolve, or at least alleviate, the security and safety problems now besetting nuclear energy, but there are no indications whether funds can be found to bring this work to commercial use. The sums involved could be as high as $15–20 billion, stretching over a period of some twenty years. Governments want companies to fund such work and companies believe that, bearing in mind the high risks involved and the long time scale, only governments have the ability to do this.

International collaboration may be a possible answer, but bearing in mind the scale of the funds needed, that is bound to involve governments. If energy were seen to be equivalent in importance to defence (as was believed during the oil crises of the 1970s), one might use the analogy of the development of new fighter aircraft. Here, collaborative deals between countries have made it possible to work on the development of a number of different aircraft, although each development might cost $30 billion or more. The deals themselves are difficult, with constant political and policy disagreements, but that is clearly seen as better than no involvement at all.

Perhaps that is the choice facing nuclear energy. Either one has international collaboration with funding from a number of governments and private organizations to develop safer reactors and a more secure fuel cycle, or we shall have to stick with the present processes, based on fifty-year-old technology, and accept that this is the only option, perhaps for centuries or until there is a serious enough accident or energy crisis for us to panic and accept, yet again, that energy security can be as important as defence. Another way of looking at the issue is to consider whether such work should be seen as worthwhile under the 'precautionary principle' agreed at the Rio Conference for combating global warming. After all, if these developments were successful, nuclear energy would be able to play a major role in this battle.

Possibly the first step in making progress with this issue is to find, or create a forum with sufficient credibility across the anti- and pro-nuclear divide to consider whether the various technological developments have a chance of resolving the problems of nuclear energy and, if so, how the work leading to commercialization might be organized and funded. The results of such deliberation would provide indications of how far nuclear energy can/should contribute to '...a safe, environmentally sound, and an economically viable energy pathway that will sustain human progress into the distant future...', as called for by the Brundtland Commission.[6]

Summary and conclusions

The following lessons can be gleaned from the analysis in this chapter.

The chapter paints a rather gloomy picture about the present status of nuclear energy. The public in many countries of the West tends to see it as unsafe, insecure, uneconomic and unnecessary and, although the public's views may be exaggerated, there is evidence for all these accusations. Yet, other countries are still very committed to this energy form while others, and especially the dynamic economies of Asia and South America, are proposing to make nuclear energy one of the cornerstones of their power generation strategy. We may, therefore, still see expansion of the industry, though with its future less and less under the control of the West.

The industry still has a number of issues, such as the destination of spent fuel and reducing the dangers of proliferation, which have to be resolved, whether the industry expands or contracts. Indeed, solution of these problems may be easier to find under conditions of expansion, as there would be greater incentive and means to do so. Under a contracting scenario there may well be pressure to leave matters to future generations or until such a time as an accident forces urgent action.

---

6 The World Commission on Environment and Development (1987), pp. 202–5.

Technological advances have shown that there is a chance of resolving many of the issues now bedevilling the nuclear industry, but for the present there are no indications that the efforts to develop these advances for commercial use will be made.

Most of the geopolitical issues identified need international action and in some instances new structures or the strengthening of present ones. The process to achieve such changes is difficult and unpopular, and there is a danger that the issues will be shelved rather than tackled.

Major expansion of nuclear power should be able to help the battle against climate change. However, it is very doubtful whether present technology could be used for such an expansion. It is more likely to provide insufficient new energy to have a significant effect on global warming, while increasing the risks of proliferation, i.e. increased danger for minimal effect.

Finally, concern has recently been expressed whether such a complex industry can continue to operate and innovate if stagnating. There are already signs that there are far fewer candidates for nuclear courses at universities and that the average age of laboratory and industry staff is increasing to middle age or higher. There is a danger that the nuclear option will close, as experience is lost and not replaced by young talent. Perhaps eastern countries will come to the rescue and provide the new expertise which the West may be unable or unwilling to develop.

Chapter 7

The rise of climate change
Michael Grubb

Introduction

One strikingly new issue to emerge into the international geopolitics of
energy since the 1970s has been concern about climate change. It is an issue
which many people are still struggling to place in the international political
and energy policy scenes; and yet it is one which could have the most profound consequences for the future of energy and which bears upon many of
the other international political issues identified in this study.

Concerns to limit carbon dioxide emissions are emerging as a diffuse
influence on other energy policy issues and decisions. The biggest
impact will be upon coal, particularly upon traded coal markets. But CO_2
limitation could also exacerbate pressures on Middle Eastern oil and
associated tensions between exporters and importers. Conversely it could
possibly enhance the international gas trade and provide a greater rational for intergovernmental cooperation in such developments, as well in
technology-oriented programmes on nuclear power and renewable energy. Climate change may also focus international debates about the rise of
Asian energy and its global implications.

This chapter addresses the issue in five sections. The first sketches the
rise of climate change as a political concern. The second section sets out
some of the broad possible implications for energy fuel mix and policy.
In the third, the chapter draws out some of the underlying political interests and influences that affect national positions. The fourth section
sketches the politics of national implementation, and the final section
outlines some of the recent political developments that underlie the current phase of negotiations.

The rise of climate change as a political concern

'Global warming' as a subject of scientific curiosity dates back to the last century. Concern in the scientific community, however, only began notice-ably to accumulate after the International Geophysical Year of 1957, which established infrastructure to begin observing and understanding planetary phenomena. By the time of the second oil shock, consciousness of climate change in academic policy circles was sufficient for it to be the subject of a detailed study by Massachusetts Institute of Technology, and it received passing reference in a 1981 study by the International Institute of Applied Systems Analysis (IIASA), entitled *Energy in a Finite World*. But no one directly involved in the great energy issues of the 1970s would have given it a second thought alongside the prominence of oil geopolitics.

At least three factors combined to change that during the 1980s. First, aided by the growth in observational evidence and computer modelling powers, the scientific evidence began to accumulate, along with some lim-ited ability to predict possible consequences. Second, in the early 1980s the UN Environment Programme teamed up with the World Meteorological Organization to arrange a series of studies and workshops aimed at build-ing a wide consensual understanding of the scientific issues, linked to pol-icy circles – efforts which came together most prominently at a series of workshops in 1987. Third, with acid rain and the ozone hole already mak-ing the headlines, the public had became sensitized to the possibility that the cumulative weight of human actions could damage the planet and its ecosystems, in ways quite different from classical local pollution issues.

By the end of 1987, therefore, the climate change issue was politically primed, and it emerged almost explosively during 1988 owing to a combi-nation of specific events.[1] To provide more authoritative analysis and

---

[1] A series of strange weather events, including an unprecedented drought in the USA, gave popular reality to the scientific images and concerns. The testimony of a leading US scientist before a Congressional committee, that climate change was probably with us, added tangible scientific weight. The perfectly timed, quasi-governmental Toronto confer-ence provided a political launch pad, with its call for a 20% reduction in CO_2 emissions by 2005. And the political East–West beauty contest to seize the high ground of new issues fol-lowing Soviet perestroika, against the intellectual background of the Brundtland report *Our Common Future*, gave high-level political authority to the wave of new concern.

advice, governments established in October 1988 the Intergovernmental Panel on Climate Change (IPCC). Its First Assessment Report in 1990 provided an in-depth appraisal along with a clear, balanced but incisive summary: one that governments around the world could understand as demonstrating that the climate change problem was real and serious. (Subsequent scientific developments, culminating in the IPCC's Second Assessment Report accepted in December 1995, have tended to reinforce the general message – see Box 7.1.) At the Second World Climate Conference of November 1990, governments accepted the report and called upon the UN to launch negotiations on a Framework Convention. The negotiations formally commenced in February 1991, and worked at breakneck pace to have a Convention ready for signing at the Rio Earth Summit in June 1992.

Following these intense efforts, the political profile of the climate change issue collapsed in exhaustion. The public was bored with the story and the media found greater interest in running sceptical challenges to the new-found and frail consensus, if they bothered with anything. Yet beneath the surface, the institutional mechanisms set in train by the IPCC and the Climate Convention continued their work, exploring the issue and its implications, and slowly gathering new force. The Convention, which by the end of the Earth Summit had already attracted more signatories than GATT, was ratified and entered into force with remarkable speed. Governments embarked upon the complex process of trying to develop policies in line with the commitments under the Convention, notably the requirement to aim at returning emissions of CO_2 and other greenhouse gases to 1990 levels by 2000, and to submit national reports on the measures taken and on emission projections.

In March/April 1995, the First Conference of the Parties to the Convention gathered in Berlin to consider the next steps, and in particular to carry out their mandated task of examining the adequacy of the existing commitments. The commitments – which ended in 2000 in terms of quantitative goals – were not adequate, they concluded. Hence was launched a new round of negotiations under the Berlin Mandate, to develop by Autumn 1997 new commitments on 'quantified limitation and reduction objectives' (emission targets) and on policies and measures, potentially out to the year 2020 (see Box 7.2).

Box 7.1 The science of climate change

Second Assessment Report of the Intergovernmental Panel on Climate Change, 1995

Key Elements of Policy-makers' Summary of the Science Working Group

Considerable progress has been made in the understanding of climate change science since 1990.

- Greenhouse gas concentrations have continued to increase as a result of human activities
- Global average surface temperature has increased:
  - by 0.3–0.6°C since the late nineteenth century;
  - recent years have been among the warmest since at least 1860;
  - the twentieth century has been warmer than any since at least 1400, prior to which reliable estimation is not possible
- The balance of evidence suggests a discernible human influence on global climate
- Best-guess estimates for changes by the year 2100, on a central (IS92a) emissions scenario, are:
  - Global average temperature rise of 2°C
  - Sea level rise of 50cm

Even if concentrations were stabilized by 2100 both temperature and sea level would continue to rise thereafter, for centuries in the case of sea level.
- Uncertainties in scenarios and sensitivities suggest ranges by 2100 of:
  - 1–3.5°C in global average temperature change
  - 15–95 cm in sea level

In all cases, the rise is predicted to be greater than any seen in the last 10,000 years, and temperatures are expected to rise more over land than at sea, and more at night than in daytime.
- Reduced thermohaline ocean circulation and an increased hydrological cycle are likely, with changes in drought and flood intensities and distributions
- Large and rapid climatic changes have occurred in the past and could occur in the future
- There are continuing major uncertainties, with most emphasis upon those concerning the behaviour of ocean currents and feedbacks associated with terrestrial ecosystems.

This decision was hard fought. Initially, such a mandate had been opposed even by the main developing countries, which feared that commitments even by the industrialized world would harm them indirectly, through trade effects, and that acknowledging the issue as a serious global issue would set them on a path that would ultimately lead them to having

Box 7.2 First Conference of Parties of the UN Framework Convention on Climate Change First session, Berlin 28 March – 7 April 1995

The 'Berlin Mandate'

1. The COP, having reviewed [the commitments] and concluded that these are not adequate, agrees to begin a process to enable it to take appropriate action for the period beyond 2000, including the strengthening of the commitments of Annex I (Industrialized) Parties ...
2. The process will, inter alia:
   (a)   Aim, as the priority in the process of strengthening the commitments – for industrialized countries, both
   * to elaborate policies and measures, as well as
   * to set quantified limitation and reduction objectives within specified timeframes, such as 2005, 2010 and 2020, for their anthropogenic emissions by sources and removals by sinks of greenhouse gases not controlled by the Montreal Protocol taking into account the differences in starting points and approaches, economic structures and resource bases, the need to maintain strong and sustainable economic growth ...
   (b)   Not introduce any new commitments for [developing countries] but reaffirm [their] existing commitments and continue to advance the implementation of these commitments in order to achieve sustainable development ...

---

to adopt binding commitments. In the run-up to (and at) Berlin, this attitude changed to reflect their own growing concern about the issue. They were also under pressure from the OPEC developing country oil exporters, who feared the impacts of constraints upon oil exports (as discussed below); but in the end OPEC lost the internal battle within the G-77 developing country group. Furthermore, industrial interests that had hitherto seemed dominated by the determination of some energy companies to halt development of the climate negotiations appeared much more fractured, with the stronger emergence of companies with the opposite concerns (such as insurance companies and 'clean' energy companies). With the pressure finally and unambiguously on the industrialized countries to move forward, it came down to an argument over words and timescales of the remit to negotiate new and more substantive commitments, and on the tone of wording regarding developing country involvement.

With the Berlin Mandate decision, and the shifts in political alignments that underlay it, climate change is now entrenched as one of the great geopolitical issues in energy. The question is whether any major government will really do anything substantive about it – and if so, what.

The policy challenge for fossil fuels

What is the role of fossil fuels in all this, and what policy options may governments pursue? The exact contribution of fossil fuels to climate change depends upon scenarios of future emissions. However, given the rapid phase-out of CFC emissions under the revisions of the Montreal Protocol, and the decline in growth rates of methane concentrations, CO_2 emissions from fossil fuels are increasingly prominent and are expected to account for about 70% of the total greenhouse-gas-induced radiative change by the end of the next century (in the IPCC's central scenario).[2]

The nature of the policy challenge for fossil fuels is defined in the first instance by the relative longevity both of CO_2 in the atmosphere, and of the energy systems that produce it. Policy will be driven in part by growing recognition that we are dealing with the interaction of two systems – the planetary and human energy systems – that are each characterized by great inertia and complexity. In such circumstances it appears rational neither to panic nor to do nothing, but rather to chart a course of sustained but not excessively costly effort to change the course of developments towards lowering emissions, while pursuing further research into the science and economics of impacts and responses. More generally, in a finite world with expanding population and economic activity, it seems almost inevitable that the relevant questions are not so much whether constraint is needed, but rather how much, when – and how.

These questions raise huge disagreements among analysts, and passionate political debates over some policy proposals, notably over carbon

---

[2]   In this (IS92a) scenario, CO_2 is estimated to account for 6W/m^2 radiative forcing by 2100, compared to 2.8 W/m^2 for all other greenhouse gas sources combined. The CO_2 figure includes deforestation, but over the next century the net contribution from deforestation is very small compared to fossil fuels. It also neglects the influence of aerosols, which are projected to make a regionally specific, highly uncertain negative contribution to radiative forcing. The scenario has been criticized for positing excessive CO_2 emissions, but the general message that CO_2 is likely to account for well over half of projected climate change appears quite robust.

tax proposals. Technically, many options can be advanced for limiting emissions. Improving the efficiency of energy systems – in conversion and end-use – has almost become a mantra of responsible policy. Though economic debates over its real potential and economics continue, there is agreement that some improvement in energy efficiency is an important part of the picture, and that at least some efficiency improvements can be encouraged by suitable government action given the many imperfections in energy markets, ranging from direct or indirect fossil fuel subsidies to the regulated monopolistic nature of most distribution networks.

Options that actually seek to affect the demand for energy services, by changing consumer behaviour or options (e.g. with respect to transport policy or infrastructure, education for energy-saving habits and lifestyles etc.) may also prove relevant over the long run, but are politically much more sensitive and have been little considered in the mainstream debate.

The other main generic option for reducing emissions is to switch between fuels. Coal is the most carbon-intensive of the fossil fuels; oil contains almost 25% less CO_2 than coal per unit of energy, and natural gas almost 25% less than oil. The total greenhouse gas emissions associated with fossil fuels are complicated by various factors: the methane content in coal mines; CO_2 contained in gas fields and methane leakage in gas transmission and distribution; and the mix of 'own use' energy consumption in the transport and (for oil) refining of the fuels. But for most sources and applications, the greenhouse gas emissions per unit of energy delivered declines markedly from coal to oil to gas, even taking account of these complications.[3]

Furthermore, the efficiency of different fuels in energy end-use varies. Most importantly, the efficiency of gas turbine combined cycle plants exceeds coal plants to such an extent that, in general, switching from coal to gas power generation can halve CO_2 emissions for the same electricity output; switching to cogeneration of heat and power, where possible and where this displaces coal or oil-based heating, can as much as halve emissions again. Figure 7.1 shows the carbon intensity of different power sources.

Then there are the non-fossil sources: nuclear, hydro, and various less

---

[3] For a detailed discussion see Grubb *et al* . (1991), Appendix II.

Figure 7.1 Carbon intensity of different power sources

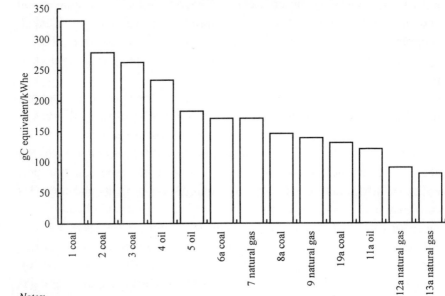

Notes:

[a] Cogeneration.
1 Average conventional steam turbine (coal)
2 Best available steam turbine (coal)
3 Pressurized fluidized bed combustion (coal)
4 Average conventional steam turbine (oil)
5 Best available combined-cycle gas turbine (oil)
6 Cogeneration: average conventional steam turbine (coal)
7 Average combined-cycle gas turbine (natural gas)
8 Cogeneration: best available steam turbine (coal)
9 Best available combined-cycle gas turbine (natural gas)
10 Cogeneration: pressurized fluidized bed combustion (coal)
11 Cogeneration: best available steam turbine (oil)
12 Cogeneration: steam-injected gas turbine (natural gas)
13 Cogeneration: best available combined-cycle gas turbine (natural gas)

Source: adapted from Grubb (1991).

widespread and less mature renewable sources. Although nuclear power does emit some CO_2 during the course of construction and fuel fabrication, for most purposes this is negligible compared to fossil fuel emissions; hydro dams may also involve greenhouse gas emissions comparable to those of nuclear energy, from construction and from decomposition in reservoirs afterwards.

One of the features of the issue so far has been the relative failure of nuclear (or hydro) power to harness political support from the climate change debate. The real winners in terms of popularity and explicitly climate-related support have been other renewable sources. This probably reflects the fact that many of the main actors driving the climate change process in the OECD at least – environmental constituencies and some environmentally inclined governments – have evolved a deep dislike and distrust of nuclear power, because of its apparent failure to deliver on promises and the legacy of difficulties sketched in the previous chapter. The nuclear industry, sensing perhaps its last chance in many countries, has sought to promote concerns about climate change, finding itself ironically alongside the 'greens'. But the signs are that, in the OECD at least, nuclear power will not receive a major boost from climate change concerns unless there are enough institutional and technical reforms to allay the inherited suspicions and remaining problems outlined in the previous chapter.

'Modernized' renewable energy sources, promoted originally on the back of concerns about oil shocks and energy security in the 1970s and 1980s, are the most obvious beneficiaries of climate-related and broader environmental concerns, particularly in Europe. The EC budget for renewable energy R&D trebled in the early 1990s, and many European countries have market supports that encourage the entry of renewables, and that, as summarized elsewhere, amount to a significant effort.[4] While the 'modernized' renewables will still amount to under 1% of European primary energy supply by the year 2000 (compared to about 4% for hydro and traditional biomass), their rapid expansion could make them quite significant on the timescales now being negotiated.[5] Renewable energy also commands pan-European support, with strong backing ffrom southern European countries. And significantly, interest extends to some key developing countries; India is the focus of major wind energy investments, and

---

[4] Grubb (1995), Chapter 7.

[5] A huge country-by-country modelling study for the European Commission's Energy Directorate suggests that renewables overall could displace an additional 110 million tonnes of CO_2 by 2010 in the 'proposed policies' scenario compared with the 'business as usual' case (180 million tonnes of CO_2 compared to 70 million tonnes of CO_2), with potentially more rapid expansion in the period 2010–20 (The European Renewable Energy Study, DG-XVII, Brussels, 1994). This compares with 1990 emissions of about 3,000 million tonnes (all figures EU-12).

aims to install 6,000MW by the year 2000, alongside significant growth of biomass and solar energy. Driven largely by the markets in Europe and India, and as a result of government responding to environmental pressures, the rate of wind energy installation globally grew at 25% per year over 1990–5.

The main 'winners', in terms of fuel sources, are thus likely to be the renewable sources and probably to some degree natural gas. Where possible, production from existing nuclear stations may be enhanced or made more profitable, and phase-outs delayed; but climate change seems unlikely to provide a nuclear renewal unless and until the industry finds a more effective basis, in terms of public and financier's trust, from which to build support. The losers are likely to be coal and, to a lesser extent, oil. The impact on conversion industries, particularly electricity, would depend upon their specific situations and regulatory structures. It is this balance of potential winners and losers arising from action to limit CO_2 emissions that underpins many aspects of the geopolitics of energy in the climate change debate.

The energy-geopolitics of climate change: defining interests

The energy-geopolitics of climate change is closely allied to, but is not identical with, the overall geopolitics of the issue. The latter involves a broader canvas that encompasses the driving concerns of small-island states, the complex politics of the timber trade, and the broader North–South debates over historical, current and future responsibilities arising from overall emissions and different levels of economic development. This chapter focuses upon the energy-related elements only – the way in which climate change is reflected in the 'new geopolitics of energy'. This section looks at the underlying interests, and perceptions of these interests, and how they influence national positions.

The distribution of emissions and intensities

The distribution of CO_2 emissions, and emissions intensity, is important because it affects national perceptions towards limiting emissions, and the political weight of and pressure on countries in the negotiations. Table 7.2 shows the distribution of CO_2 emissions in 1990, and as

**Table 7.2 Distribution of world carbon dioxide emissions, 1990, and
projections by International Energy Agency (billion tonnes CO2)**

	1990	2000 ES	2000 CC	2010 ES	2010 CC
OECD	10.4	11.1	11.6	11.6	12.9
North America	5.6	6.0	6.4	6.2	6.9
Europe	3.4	3.5	3.6	3.7	4.1
Pacific	1.4	1.6	1.6	1.7	1.9
FSU/CEE	5.2	3.3	3.5	3.8	4.4
RoW	6.0	8.8	8.9	12.8	13.4
China	2.4	3.5	3.5	5.1	5.1
Other East Asia	0.9	1.6	1.6	2.3	2.5
South Asia	0.7	1.1	1.1	1.8	2.0
Other	2.0	2.6	2.7	3.6	3.8
World	21.6	23.2	24.1	28.2	30.7

Source: IEA (1995d).

projected to the years 2000 and 2010 by the International Energy Agency
for two scenarios ('energy savings', and 'capacity constraints').

Figure 7.2 shows a graphical illustration of the distribution in 1993 from
a different perspective, namely in terms of emissions per capita compared
against population (the product – the area of the blocks – is thus proportion-
al to total emissions). The USA was the biggest emitter, accounting for 25%
of the global total; the countries of central/eastern Europe, including Russia,
in total accounted for another 17%, but following the break-up and economic contraction of this region, the European Union is left as the second biggest
cohesive economic group, emitting almost 16% of global CO_2 emissions
(including the new members). Emissions from developing countries are rising rapidly, and now account for over a quarter of the global total.

On a per capita basis, the USA is again the most profligate emitter and
forms a distinct group along with Canada and Australia; European per
capita emissions are in a range similar to Japan and (now) to the former
USSR, at about half this level. On this measure there is a big gulf compared with most developing countries, where emissions per capita are typ-
ically several times lower than in developed countries.

Figure 7.2 Emissions per capita and population, 1993

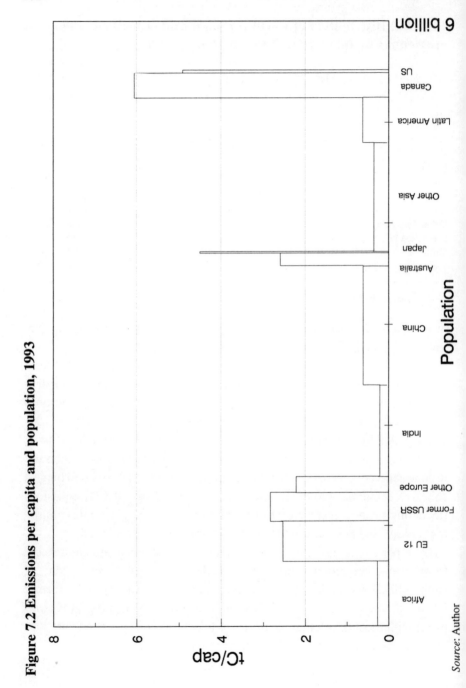

Source: Author

Because of this and differences in wealth, and the fact that the developed countries have dominated emissions historically, developing countries have taken the attitude that stabilization of emissions from industrialized countries is a precondition for them to consider any substantive abatement action.

The economic collapse of the former Soviet Union means that emissions are contracting there anyway, and precludes them from taking a more active position; there is little sign that climate change politics has become important there yet, and the collapse of emissions since the late 1980s has made it easy for these countries to achieve the Convention's interim aim. Nevertheless, one can speculate on how energy resource endowments will affect national attitudes and internal debate. Notably, Gazprom could engage west European concerns about climate change in support of increased gas exports, but maintaining internal consistency would require struggling with the coal and oil interests in Russia. In the rest of central and eastern Europe, the situation is even more complex, with concern about excessive dependence on Russian energy providing conflicting incentives depending in part upon domestic coal or non-fossil fuel endowments.

At present, however, much of this is speculative. Most central and east European countries are still in the process of transition, and the real focus is upon the OECD countries that currently account for about half of global CO_2 emissions.

Positions in the OECD

Europe The European Union as an institution, and many of its members (now including the environmentally sensitive countries of Sweden, Austria and Finland), have called for action almost ever since the issue emerged politically. The north European countries, in particular have a relatively strong perception of international and environmental responsibility, and sympathy with developing countries. Except for the UK and Norway, all are net energy importers. In many, environmental issues gained prominence during the 1980s, notably over acid rain and ozone depletion – dismissed as scaremongering at the beginning of the decade, and recognized as major

Box 7.3 Climate change politics in Northern Europe

Germany, by virtue of its economic weight and the rhetorical force of its stance on climate change, has been at the heart of European climate change politics. Sensitized by the acid rain experience and galvanized by the political success of the Green Party, the German position has since the late 1980s sought to lead European and international action. Its target of 25–30% reduction in CO_2 emissions by 2005, reiterated by Chancellor Kohl at Berlin in 1995, is by far the most ambitious of any major country; its hosting of the Berlin conference, and successful bid for Bonn to host the new Climate Change Secretariat, highlight its continuing aspirations on the issue. As discussed below in considering implementation, the reality is, however, not simple; its two smaller neighbours, *the Netherlands* and *Denmark*, can claim equal commitment with somewhat greater consistency, but lack the political weight of Germany.

France and *Italy* play a more ambiguous role, but at the level of the EU Council of Environment Ministers they have tended to support the German stance. The accession in 1995 of Austria and the environmentally sensitive Scandinavian countries has further increased the weight of countries disposed to take a strong stance on environmental issues, including climate change.

The UK and *Norway* occupy rather special positions. The UK in 1990 was still scarcely in the fold in terms of European climate change attitudes; indeed it was the UK, already being halfway across the Atlantic, that brokered the US–EC compromise that underpins the Convention's Article 4.2 on commitments. Since then, however, the collapse of the UK coal industry and the leadership of UK science in the IPCC have combined to move the UK decisively into the European fold in terms of underlying attitudes to climate change, though political resistance to EU-led action will remain potent.

In Norway the situation is rather different. There was never much question about Norway's environmental or internationalist credentials, but it has run into the reality that the peculiar structure of its energy economy, and Norway's role as mainstream and growing provider of European oil and gas, makes stabilization of its own CO_2 emissions a virtual impossibility. Norway can only play a productive role in climate change as an integrated part of the European effort, and unless novel approaches are adopted, the referendum rejection of EU membership puts a seal on that. Outside the Union's efforts, the manifest inability of Mrs Brundtland's country to stabilize emissions, though tiny in global terms and thoroughly explicable, is symbolically damaging to the whole negotiating process. Norway in turn complains about the irony that a major part of its problem – the growth of emissions related to gas exports against a hydro-based power sector (some of which is also exported) – in fact contributes to reducing emissions elsewhere in Europe. Thus Norway needs the Union; and the Union needs Norway. As yet, however, no institutional structure has been developed, or even seriously proposed, to reap the political benefits of formalizing cooperation between Norway and the Union on the goals and policies of climate change.

threats justifying belated and sometimes expensive action by the end of the decade, an experience that has led to elaboration of the 'precautionary principle' to environmental policy. Many of these countries also sense economic reasons for action, both in terms of the benefits of improved energy efficiency, and the technological leadership, a view expounded most pointedly by the Delors White Paper on Competitiveness.[6]

Of course, EU member countries vary with respect to various economic and institutional factors; indeed some of the problems faced by the EU reflect those that could arise, on a larger scale, at the global level in the negotiation of a coordinated climate change strategy. There is a 'North–South' dimension, with four countries in a markedly less advanced development stage: the poorer 'Cohesion' countries[7] do not want to bear the responsibility for past emissions of other EU countries, and they fear any constraint on energy consumption as an obstacle to the main aim of economic growth. Climate policy declarations in the EU have recognized the disparity, and that emissions from these countries are likely to grow in the context of overall stabilization, requiring reductions from some other member states if the EU target is to be achieved (discussed below). Specific positions are outlined in Box 7.3.

The United States and Canada In contrast to Europe, the USA has until recently been more hesitant about the climate change issue overall and has expressed grave fears about the economic consequences of CO_2 abatement, along with doubts about the 'precautionary principle'. Apart from specific political circumstances, one source of resistance is the US's pattern of economic development based upon low-price domestic fossil fuels. It is the largest coal producer and the second largest producer of oil and natural gas. One analyst concluded with acerbity that 'the history of US energy demand and the existing resources, infrastructure and institutions make the US economy as dependent upon fossil fuels as a heroin addict is on the needle'.[8] This feeds into the perception, widespread in the US, that

---

[6] *Growth, Competitiveness and Employment*, Commission of the European Communities, Brussels/Luxembourg, 1993

[7] Spain, Portugal, Greece and Ireland.

[8] Rayner, 'The Greenhouse Effect in the US: the Legacy of Energy Abundance', in Grubb *et al.* (1991), p. 277.

the costs of reducing CO_2 emissions would be very high, and hundreds of millions of dollars have been spent on economic analysis that supports this perspective (in contrast to Europe, where more money has been spent on economic studies that support the opposite conclusion).[9] The relative iso-lationism of the USA, especially from the developing world, has also made it easier to divert attention from its domestic energy consumption by point-ing to the role of other sources (such as deforestation and rice cultivation) and of developing country growth, with limited comprehension of the forces and perceptions involved.

The US position has evolved. The political influence of the scientific sceptics declined after the publication of the first IPCC assessment (and was more or less buried by the Second Assessment Report). In the Convention negotiations there was an emphasis on the contribution of existing environmental and energy policies (including the 1990 Clean Air Act, and the National Energy Strategy). The election of the Clinton administration including the environmentalist Vice-President Al Gore, produced a big change in the rhetoric, with commitment to a national action programme and a goal of returning overall greenhouse gas emis-sions to 1990 levels by 2000. But the decline in media attention every-where took an extreme form in the USA, with almost nothing surfacing during the period from the Earth Summit until mid-1995 other than occa-sional sceptical claims about the science and scare stories about extreme costs of abatement. Furthermore, with the Congressional system acting to protect the interests of coal-producing states and oil and electricity companies, Congress exercises a virtual stranglehold on what can be implemented; achieving the climate plan is still largely in doubt.

---

[9]   The 1990 Economic Report of the President put the costs of reducing US CO_2 emissions by 20% at between \$800bn and \$3.6tn, based on the modelling work of A.S. Manne and R.G. Richels, 'CO_2 emission limits: an economic cost analysis for the USA', *Energy, the International Journal*, April 1990. A broad review of economic modelling studies is given in M. Grubb, J. Edmonds *et al.*, 'The economic costs of limiting fossil fuel CO_2 emissions: a survey and analysis', *Annual Review of Energy and Environment*, Annual Reviews Inc, Palo Alto, 1993; and in Chapters 8 and 9 of the IPCC Second Assessment, Working Group III Report.

However, the Clinton/Gore administration remains committed to action, and public concern is rising. The 1995 IPCC assessment was almost the first thing to break through the US media for three years, in particular its conclusion that climate change was being observed (a conclusion that was based heavily upon pattern-matching work in US government laboratories – a testament to the strength and integrity of US science). Given the fickle nature and power of US public opinion, a major swing of the pendulum in terms of the US position cannot be entirely ruled out – though implementation in such a federal, lobbied system with a resource-based economy will always be problematic. However, the USA may emerge to support a 'strong law' emissions protocol, as something that would fit better with its legalistic system and flush out the real extent of European commitment.

The situation in Canada, despite its strongly environmentalist rhetoric in the period before Rio, has been similar: a resource-based economy with still-expanding population and industrial economy, in a highly federal system, Canada has become noticeably quiet about the issue of climate change.

Japan   The position of Japan is more ambiguous. Japan joined the international trend and adopted a delicately worded two-tier CO_2 emission target in 1990, and it has continued to seek a middling position, which reflects scarcely concealed intense internal debates. Japan is already probably the most energy-efficient country in the world, especially in its industrial sector, and so may have greater difficulty than others in meeting equivalent emission targets. Also, Japan shows little direct concern about possible climate change impacts, and has not traditionally been one of the more 'internationalist' countries.

But there are also strong contrary factors. With an economy wholly dependent upon imported fossil fuels, 'CO_2 constraints are perceived as an opportunity for Japan to revitalise energy conservation and other policies which are desirable in and of themselves'.[10] Japan exudes technological confidence, and is seeking an international political profile to match its economic might. Barred by its constitution from contributing to international peacekeeping efforts, in the early 1990s debate about Japan's

---

[10] Tanabe and Grubb, 'The Greenhouse Effect in Japan: Burden or Opportunity?', in Grubb *et al.* (1991), p. 281.

'*Kokusai koken*' (international contribution) turned towards environmental issues as an area where Japan could play its rightful role as a mature and responsible international player, leading the world into a sustainable twenty-first century.[11]

Japan has thus sought routes to export efficient technology and production processes to developing countries (particularly to the East Asian newly industrialized countries), both as a political and as a commercial exercise. Like Germany, Japan senses commercial advantages in a CO_2-constrained world – advantages enhanced by getting in first. In November 1995, MITI led a high-level visit to India, pursuing an initiative to provide a demonstration efficient steel plant under the rubric of 'activities implemented jointly'.

The position of Australia, the world's largest coal exporter, again illustrates the importance of energy and economic interests: despite a strong environmental movement it has, like Canada, withdrawn to a cautious position on the climate change issue.

Thus, the position of OECD countries is a complex network of resource-based interests and historically acquired attitudes towards environment, technology and internationalism. This underlies the difficult problem of how to distribute the effort internationally, in ways that are reasonably fair and politically feasible, which is intimately bound up with energy interests and energy politics even within the OECD, let alone beyond it. The Convention simply sidesteps this by defining the same interim aim for all industrialized countries. For commitments beyond 2000 this is certainly inefficient, and perhaps unfeasible. The question of whether and how to differentiate commitments, as part of overall strategy towards sharing the effort, is an immediate and central political dilemma.

Developing country energy exporters

After the 'North–South' divide, probably the deepest division in climate change is that between major energy exporters and others. The most overt expression of energy exporter concerns has emerged in the efforts of

---

[11] Yasuko Kawashima, personal communication; presentation to Consultative Workshop on QELROS, Geneva, 28 February 1996.

OPEC countries, notably Saudi Arabia and Kuwait, to impede the climate change negotiations since their inception, and in their vitriolic objections to the EC carbon tax proposals. Their concern is understandable. These countries' foreign earnings depend almost entirely upon oil exports, and soft oil prices since the heady days of the 1970s combined with high military expenditures (including repayments for the 1990–1 war) have left them financially pressured. For the longer term, Saudi Arabia and Kuwait above all have sought to keep oil prices moderate so as to maintain buoyant long-term oil demand, in which they would be dominant suppliers. From this perspective, climate change is a threat to their entire resource strategy and long-term prospects.

In addition to their general concerns about the potential impact of efforts to limit CO_2 emissions, these countries have focused concerns about one particular proposed instrument. At a time of weak oil prices, they have perceived carbon tax proposals in a simple light: as an attempt by the importers to seize yet more of the rents from oil. And they reacted accordingly, with ferocious opposition to the EC proposals in particular, contributing, albeit marginally, to their demise. But neither oil exporters nor US industrial interests have succeeded in halting the broader process of climate change negotiations, as set out in the final part of this chapter.

Asian advance

The Asian developing countries overall accounted for about 22% of global fossil fuel CO_2 emissions in 1990, according to the IEA (Table 7.2); the Japan Institute of Energy Economics estimates that Asia–APEC excluding Japan accounted for 15% in 1992. Because of their growth rates, these countries occupy a pivotal place in thinking about climate change in the next century. China and India alone account for almost 40% of the current and projected world population; and as sketched in Chapter 5 of this book, energy demand is growing explosively in both countries and coal is widely considered to be the prime fossil fuel resource. The IEA *Energy Outlook* suggests that Asia overall (excluding

Japan) will account for about 30% of global CO_2 emissions by 2010; the JIEE projections suggest that Asia-APEC (excluding Japan) will account for about 22%.[12] At the projected expansion rates, by 2020 Chinese emissions could match those projected for the USA, and Asian emissions overall could match those projected for the OECD (author's extrapolation from projections to 2010).

The future attitudes and options of these countries towards climate change is therefore crucial; and it is enigmatic. The popular image in the West, that they simply have no concern at all about the climate issue, is not correct. Many prominent Chinese scientists are very worried about the impact of climate change upon China's dense coast- and river-based population, and China has encouraged the participation of some of its leading researchers in both climate science and analysis of response options. India has several of the world's leading research centres on energy issues, with a strong focus on climate change research, and India leads the developing world in its encouragement of renewable energy developments, with rapidly growing investments in a number of renewable sources.

But these countries undoubtedly fear the economic consequences of any emission constraints and have a deep sense of equity issues emanating from the huge international disparities in emissions and wealth. India often assumes a radical leadership position of developing countries in North–South debates, and on several occasions has done so on climate change, emphasizing that developing countries will never do anything that constricts their development. China, with a growing sense of its market power and paradoxical power from potential emissions, has made it plain that it will not be pushed into anything it feels unhappy with.

To these countries (and most of the developing world) the first principle is quite simple: nothing should stand in the way of economic development, and they cannot consider substantive action on climate change until the OECD has demonstrated clear leadership responsibilities by getting its own emissions under control, and willingness to compensate developing countries for any efforts they make to follow suit. This contrasts sharply with the tone of debate in the USA where, as indicated, the emphasis is

---

[12] International Energy Agency (1995e); Japan Institute of Energy Economics (1995).

upon the fact that any OECD constraint could be swamped by growth in the developing world, hence casting doubts on whether to take action unless the developing countries are also involved.

The biggest future impacts on emissions, not inappropriately, will thus to an important degree be determined by the political dynamic between the three largest coal-based economies in the world.

The only bridge across this aspect of the 'North–South' divide to be seriously pursued so far is that of joint implementation (JI), which in its purest form represents the idea that companies or governments in the industrialized world could reduce emissions in developing countries and credit the emission savings to their own accounts. This proposal itself raised a furore, with concerns about equity, control and ease of monitoring fuelling developing country opposition. The Berlin conference reached a compromise agreement on a pilot phase of 'activities implemented jointly' (without any credits) and specific projects are cumulating, with 27 JI projects under way as of April 1996. However, the impact of JI so far is entirely negligible in comparison with the explosion of investment in conventional coal and oil production and power technologies in developing countries.

The politics of implementation and credibility

Despite all the international discussion and expressions of concern and commitment, few countries have yet really succeeded in integrating climate change concerns beyond the fringes of energy policy and major energy investment decisions. Several OECD countries are unlikely to meet the targets in the Convention, and it remains unclear how far pressures developed from the international negotiations will transmit through national political systems. The reality is that many people involved in climate change have never understood the complexities and competing objectives associated with energy policy, and many of those involved in energy policy have never taken very seriously the objective of limiting CO_2 emissions. The wagon of international negotiations thus risks leaving the realities of implementation behind.

This is most clearly illustrated by the gulf between declarations and implementation in the most ambitious major country, Germany. On the surface the German national programme appears extensive, listing no fewer than 130 measures being taken to limit emissions. Yet on closer inspection, most of these are minor, and most were developed for other reasons, having been subsequently highlighted because they may also limit greenhouse gas emissions. None of the measures described seems likely to make a big impact on German CO_2 emissions. The only really substantive measure to be strongly advanced was the CO_2 tax proposal, transmuted to an energy tax to avoid excessive impact on coal, which was then made conditional upon the EU tax, which any astute observer could tell was a political impossibility from early 1993 at the latest. The leading SDP opposition party embraced it on paper, with the ludicrous exception that it should not apply at all to coal – the production of which continues to be subsidized, though at a declining level, to 2005. In fact, the existing commitments on coal production, combined with failure (as elsewhere) to tackle transport growth, make it clear that Germany will not get anywhere near the targeted 25% emissions reduction. Presumably to avoid public admission of this embarrassing fact, at the time of writing Germany remains the only OECD country technically in violation of the Convention, by refusing to produce a CO_2 emission projection for 2000. Limiting CO_2 emissions in Germany is an important objective – it just happens to be not as important as other objectives that involve maintaining CO_2 emissions (despite the fact that coal subsidies actually penalize the German economy). The Environment Ministry cannot change this, because it involves interests and responsibilities that lie outside environmental policy.

The German situation is extreme, but few countries have implemented as much as they appeared to promise at Rio. The European Commission announced in March 1996 that it hoped to achieve the overall stabilization target for 2000 (though some further measures might be necessary),[13] and Japan expects to achieve its per capita (but not

---

[13] European Commission, *Second Report under the Monitoring Decision*, EC DG-XI, Brussels, March 1996. The results of this assessment, announced to the Ad-Hoc Group on the Berlin Mandate on 4 March 1996, are projected on the basis of member states' submissions and Commission analysis that the total CO_2 emissions from the European Union in 2000 would be in the range 0–5% above 1990 levels in the absence of a carbon tax, and stated that other kinds of additional measures could be brought forward to achieve the stabilization goal if it proves necessary.

absolute) target, but the outlook in the USA is much less promising and several smaller countries (Canada, Australia, New Zealand and Norway) clearly will be wide of the mark. It is politically significant that if the EU does achieve its goal as now claimed, it will mean that most industrialized countries do achieve the target they signed up to at Rio.[14] But even in those that do, critics can point out that most of the progress is attributable to factors other than climate policy – whether it is German reunification, economic transformation in Eastern Europe, or privatization of the UK electricity supply system.

It would not be accurate to describe the lack of implementation as an impasse, or even a failure to introduce meaningful 'climate policies'. The problem lies partly in the fact that the issue arose against a background of 'environmental problems' in which it was possible to consider solutions separately from overall energy policy: specifying clean-up technologies or processes, or otherwise imposing requirements that led industry to bear the costs of implementing clean-up. Climate change is far more complex, because it is intimately bound up with overall energy policy. The bigger 'climate change policies' considered to date cannot be driven and implemented by pressure just from a discrete climate change lobby, or an environment ministry.

So will governments do anything serious? The classical argument among political sceptics is that CO_2 constraints will impede economic growth, and that governments will never be able to agree how to distribute or implement the painful measures required. In this author's view this is a misreading of the issue. Rather, climate change is becoming part of the broader process of coalition politics that dominates big decisions in any democracy. Policies that limit CO_2 emissions substantially are likely to be part of a package that attracts a range of other interests. Frequently, climate

---

[14] Fifteen countries are covered under the EU 'umbrella' target, and the Convention commitments are deliberately structured to allow the aim to be met jointly in this manner; the Cohesion countries, France and some others made it plain that they only signed the Convention under this provision, and thus can claim compliance if the EU achieves the goal collectively. In addition, all the central and east European countries will have CO_2 emissions in 2000 below the 1990 levels. Strictly speaking, therefore, about 80% of Annex 1 countries will be able to claim compliance with the interim aim.

change has been a modest influence upon the outcome of decisions that had to be faced anyway. Most of the elements in the UK's national climate programme, for example, can be traced to coalitions that involve other interests, whether it is the tax-raising interests of the Treasury, the political imperative towards privatization and weakening of trade unions (particularly coal), or the social concerns of the fuel-poverty lobby to see poor homes better insulated.

Thus in many countries climate change is emerging as a diffuse influence upon other decisions, rather than a discrete policy; one that pushes decisions in the direction of lower carbon and the promotion of measures to improve energy efficiency and clean energy technologies. The strength of this influence will be determined by scientific developments, popular perception, media concerns, the strength and ability of environment ministries, and the progress in negotiations. The extent to which the development of international law increases the governmental commitment will in turn depend upon resolution of some of the political problems noted above, which will determine whether governments feel there is a fair and meaningful sharing of the effort.

Overall, the pressures and actions to limit CO_2 emissions are building up. Such a cumulation of small measures, perhaps growing into stronger measures as the institutional reach of climate concerns grows and the negotiations proceed, may have a substantial long-run impact. But for a long time, the politics of implementation, and the credibility with which countries can really deliver on promises they make, will come under increasing scrutiny as the international negotiations proceed.

Conclusions

Of all the new issues in the geopolitics of energy, climate change has erupted most rapidly and strikingly. The political history of the issue, rising from virtual obscurity in the spring of 1988 to the Berlin Mandate seven years later and followed by the IPCC's Second Assessment Report, points to a breadth and depth of concern that is now institutionalized in a way that might provide a base for a substantial political force.

However, it is still far from clear to what extent this will be realized in actual energy policy. Few countries have yet really succeeded in integrating climate change concerns beyond the fringes of energy policy and major energy investment decisions. Although the majority of industrialized countries will probably achieve the interim stabilization aim set out in the Convention, for many this is incidental and several OECD countries are unlikely to achieve it.

Climate change policy faces the general political challenge of broadening the constituency for action, in two dimensions. One is international: to develop a regime which involves a definition and distribution of commitment that is perceived to be both fair and effective. This is needed to give countries assurance that they will not be losing out relative to competitors, and that their efforts will not be futile, swamped by the rise of developing country emissions. The other dimension is internal: to integrate climate concerns with the broader web of energy policy and economic decision-making.

If and as the pressures and actions to limit CO_2 emissions do combine to have a substantial long-run impact, they will directly influence the other geopolitical energy issues set out in this study. The biggest impact will be on coal, which has a relatively low geopolitical profile and which has not been much explored here. But to the extent that climate policies focus on and reduce oil consumption, they will amplify the already considerable pressure on the Middle East sketched in Chapter 3 – at least unless such policies are complemented by measures to restrict the continued expansion of non-OPEC production which, as set out in Chapter 2, has considerable pace and force behind it.

Conversely, to the extent that climate policies act to accelerate the growth of natural gas (particularly in power generation), this may also accelerate the emergence of Russia as an energy superpower, and perhaps provide an added incentive to try to pursue multilateral collaboration to develop Russia's resources for Asia. And climate concerns further put the spotlight on Asian energy prospects, particularly raising questions about coal as the solution to Asia's energy security concerns. Finally, climate change concerns represent a new, global rationale for nuclear power, but the signs are that this only further highlights the need to find forms of nuclear technology and organization that are publicly acceptable, and more generally the need for coherent international collaboration in the development of both better nuclear and renewable energy technologies.

The projection of climate policy on to the geopolitics of energy is mirrored by the projection of energy policy on to the geopolitics of climate change negotiations, where it heralds possible new alliances and new potentials for confrontation. The historical divide between the USA and European energy policy is likely to be extended into the broader questions of environmental responsibilities and resource profligacy, with Japan potentially in a mediating role. In the central and east European countries, Gazprom could seek to ride the climate issue by promoting gas exports while former client states debate the merits and costs of reducing dependence on Russian energy, with competing implications for attitudes towards climate change.

Outside the industrialized countries, the tension between energy exporters (particularly OPEC) and importers (particularly the USA and Japan, but also developing country importers) could be seriously exacerbated, unless the combination of climate change with the traditional oil agenda allows some meaningful compromise to be found in the moribund producer–consumer dialogue. And the general shift of energy issues towards Asia is likely to be reflected in climate change, as the debate focuses increasingly upon questions of Chinese and Indian coal, and the prospects for developing alternatives.

Such are the energy-geopolitics of climate change. Berlin opened the gates to a potentially much more substantive climate change regime, and this chapter has sketched some of the possible implications and likely positions. Whether and how such issues materialize, in the next steps at least, is likely to depend more upon the politics of national implementation than upon the grand heights of international diplomacy.

Chapter 8

Conclusions

This chapter discusses the new geopolitical agenda, the process by which it is addressed, the role of energy administrations and energy policies, and finally suggests some 'projects' by which the present and future energy issues may contribute to wider international cooperation and understanding: a contrast to the divisive and confrontational issues of the 'old' agenda.

Geopolitics and energy

The conditions which propelled the policies and attitudes of 'energy crises' into international geopolitics no longer hold: governments almost everywhere have withdrawn or are withdrawing from detailed economic management including management of energy demand and investment. The exceptions – the key oil exporting countries of the Middle East – face a diminished role in the world energy and oil markets: their growing revenue requirements are unlikely to be satisfied by increasing prices or large increases in export volumes in the next decade or more. Their problems are increased, and they are divided, by sanctions imposed on some of them for geopolitical reasons. Though the risks of temporary disruptions to oil supplies are increasing as a result of these pressures, the ability of oil and energy markets to mitigate those disruptions has dramatically improved over the past fifteen years. The geopolitical options are also wider, as a result of the end of the Cold War, the temporary economic weakness of Russia and the development of the Middle East peace process. There are new players in both the energy and geopolitical games: East Asia as a market for energy, China as a power extending its influence and authority, Russia as an economy whose energy industries are increasingly being integrated with international markets. Nuclear power has been marginalized in many countries. Climate change has become an international issue of increasing political importance and with energy consequences. The new agenda reflects these new realities. Broad policies – economic liberalization, national development, independence, foreign policy and security – affect the arithmetic of energy supply; the arithmetic of energy supply affects, but is generally subordinate to, these broad policies. That is the message of the previous chapters.

Oil production outside the Middle East

Policies of national development in much of the world – now including the former Soviet Union and China – are being enhanced by economic reforms: liberalization, and the withdrawal of governments from enterprise management. These policies have an international dimension because they involve integration with world trade and financial markets. Part of their success comes from the benefits brought by access to finance, markets, technology, management and efficiency driven by international competition. These effects apply in the energy sector also, to make the development of petroleum supplies ever easier, ever more competitive, and ever more diverse . Oil production outside OPEC and the former Soviet Union has expanded steadily for thirty years and is likely to continue to expand steadily to 2010 (the horizon of this book). Figure 2.5 illustrated this prospect vividly. The near-term policy questions are:

- How will far economic liberalization reach into the petroleum sector of countries such as Mexico, Brazil and China, which have substantial potential for expanding oil production capacity?
- What measures are available to oil-importing countries to support and encourage that process through facilitating the flow of investment and technology to those countries where the oil is?

The Middle East

The result of the present trends makes grim arithmetic for the Middle East OPEC oil exporters. Their share of world oil production is likely to remain at around 30% to 2010 and the demand for their oil may not rise before

2000. In all exporters except Saudi Arabia, revenue will continue to fall behind the growth of population and their aspirations.

In the Middle East, more than anywhere else, petroleum development is the creature of wider, non-petroleum policies and conflicts. The oil exporting countries are rivals in almost every dimension. They compete for influence among themselves, over borders, for influence in the Arab and Islamic worlds, and on the Middle East peace process which currently embodies the long-term US commitment (for non-petroleum reasons) to Israel. Petroleum policies express this rivalry. Petroleum export revenues, on which their economies and government budgets depend, are these countries' principal economic weapon against one another. Petroleum revenue in the long run depends on expanding production capacity and defending market share. Revenue in the short term depends on moderating this competition so that the price does not collapse.

Over the past twenty years the competitive-collaborative mechanism has shifted from the compromises of a 'cartel' approach to the manoeuvres of a 'dominant supplier' as Saudi Arabia has gained share dramatically (see Figure 3.7). This shift to Saudi Arabia is not fully explained by oil arithmetic (all the exporters have some potential to expand output and capacity). The explanation lies in much more profound differences. All the countries concerned reject, to some extent, foreign influences and trends, but they have chosen to reject different things.

In broad terms, Saudi Arabia has chosen to reject foreign ideas of democracy and human rights (including women's rights) but has found an effective way of working with foreign enterprises to absorb technology, management and investment in the development of its oil-based economy. Through its membership of the IMF governing body it plays an identifiable part in the international financial system. It has also found a way of securing foreign commitments to protect its national security, and these have been shown to work.

The Islamic Republic of Iran since 1979 has vigorously pursued a very broad programme of rejection of things modern and foreign (though it has maintained and even strengthened the evolution of an elective parliamentary system and, unlike Saudi Arabia, publishes comprehensive economic and budgetary data).Those rejections have put Iran, unlike Saudi Arabia, into confrontation with much of the international community on matters such as the hostage-taking in Tehran, the *fatwa* on Salman Rushdie, the harassment of tankers in the Gulf, alleged support for international terrorism, and an interest in developing access to nuclear technology and potential weapons fuel, to name but a few. The Republic has also confronted its neighbours on new ideological issues as well as old frontier disputes.

Iraq has rejected a different selection from the menu of modernism and contemporary international relations. It has rejected any constraints on furthering national interests by aggressive war whenever the opportunity appears to offer and with whatever weapons can be obtained.

Foreign responses to the differentiated menus of rejection have differentiated accordingly. Saudi Arabia has access to foreign technology, management, finance, markets, and (not least) military protection. Foreign economic interests in Iran are limited by a variety of difficult conditions, not least of which are the US sanctions. It is a nominal objective of the present regime in Iraq to use foreign technology and finance to reverse more than 25 years of confrontation and exclusion of foreign firms so that they can be used to rebuild and expand Iraq's petroleum sector. Foreign companies' interest cannot be tested in earnest because of the UN sanctions. Neither Iraq nor Iran has military allies in the region (or elsewhere). The ability (or willingness) of Russia to offer practical help is limited by Russian economic weakness, a backlog of unpaid bills, and the trade-off against other Russian foreign interests – such as relationships with the USA.

The US policy of 'dual containment' of Iraq and Iran is a precise and well-defined expression of a much wider set of foreign responses to the rejectionism practised by those two countries. Given the long history and deep roots of this rejectionism, it is not likely to change fast and convincingly, and nor are the responses to it.

The implication for the petroleum sector is that the long-run expansion of petroleum capacity will continue to be dominated – and to some extent managed – by the oil policy of Saudi Arabia, which in turn depends on that country's continuing to differentiate itself from the other producers in its relations with the world outside the Middle East. This carries immense short-term risks: Saudi Arabia could be disrupted, as Iran was in 1978, by internal contradictions in its particular 'menu of rejectionism'. The other countries could be disrupted – or driven again to aggression – by the urgency of their economic problems.

For the energy calculus, the key conclusions of the Middle Eastern section of the geopolitical agenda are simple:

- Rivalry between the Middle East oil exporters, combined with their vast overhang on undeveloped petroleum reserves, will ensure the continued expansion of supply – probably ahead of demand – for many decades.
- The tensions within and between Middle East oil exporters, and between some of them and the rest of the world, will continue to create instability and the risk of temporary disruptions in supply and investment.
- Decisions on the geopolitical agenda lie primarily within the Middle East itself. Though the details change, the Middle East story continues to be a saga of competitive expansion with political interruptions. The policies that matter are the broad choices of Middle Eastern countries about the nature of their societies and the range and depth of their connections with the other countries:
  - Can individual countries maintain their stability in a scenario where there is no rising trend in oil prices, and development of volume is slow?
  - Will there be any change in the policies of 'rejectionism' which at present place two major producers in conflict with much of the rest of the world on so many issues?

These choices, and foreign responses to them, determine the nature and degree of their competition for oil revenues.

Russia/CIS

In Russia and also the rest of the former Soviet Union, the energy arithmetic falls out of a much larger dynamic of change in almost every political and economic parameter: border, constitution, economic structure, the organization of society, relations with the rest of the world, are simultaneously in transition. The collapse of the former system has foreclosed many options, but there are still choices to be made in those countries about the timing, degree and precise form by which democratic government, civil society and a market economy will develop. These broad developments have three outcomes which affect the energy sector and which are not driven by energy objectives:

- The decentralization and vertical integration of the oil sector, setting its privatized companies on the road to integration in, and competition within, the international oil industry and financial markets.
- By contrast, a greater role for Gazprom as the manager of both the domestic and export gas industry, distanced by privatization from direct government control and by the disappearance of the Communist system from day-to-day political party management.
- The development of an internal energy market in which investment decisions and fuel choices will increasingly respond to market forces – albeit imperfect ones.

The results in the energy field will be an eventual resumption of growth in oil production and a continued expansion of gas production and export. The scale and timing will depend as much on how quickly, and in precisely what final form, all the conditions come together for long-term investment (whether by Russian or foreign investors).

For other former Soviet energy producers – Kazakhstan, Azerbaijan and Turkmenistan – similar internal policies of political and economic reform will frame energy development policies. These countries have the added complication of their relationships with Russia, which controls many of their potential energy export routes and presents a wider agenda of issues to be resolved: the treatment of Russian populations, the security of the borders of the former Soviet Union, and the challenge of reducing the economic support from Russia which these countries enjoyed in Soviet times.

As with the Middle East, the theme is that very large petroleum potential will be developed at a time and in a form determined by broader political and economic considerations. The new element, not confined to the energy industries, is the degree of integration with international markets for fuels, finance and technology and the role of internal markets in allocating resources. The geopolitical agenda is about:

- Continuing the process of economic reform and strengthening the institutions of civil society in Russia and the other successors to the former Soviet Union.
- The broad economic and security relationship between Russia and western Europe, whose energy markets can potentially be expanded by further supplies of Russian gas.
- The total political relationship between Russia and former Soviet states which are either large potential energy producers (Azerbaijan, Kazakhstan, Turkmenistan) or important transit countries for Russia (Ukraine and Belarus).

East Asia

In East Asia the unfolding of economic reform in China, combined with the policies supporting continuation of rapid economic growth in other countries of the region, generates the prospect of rapidly increasing energy demand.

The energy arithmetic suggests that this demand will increasingly be met by imports from outside the region. The same liberal and trade-oriented policies will generate, through economic success, the resources to meet that demand by imports from the international market.

Growth generates its own security problems. To an extent long forgotten in Europe or the USA, governments in East Asia are concerned about the continuous rapid expansion of energy supplies to support their economic growth. Where domestic resources exist, their development (with a little foreign technology here and there) can be made more certain by the use of foreign resources.

Gas for East Asia can offer secure expansion of supply because both LNG and gas pipeline projects require long-term commitments by supplier and importer alike, but these commitments will be difficult to construct across borders. To raise gas from its present low share in the East Asia energy market in the long term requires that various broad policy issues be resolved to open the way for pipeline exports from Russia: these depend

on the general political and economic relationship between China and
Russia, on whether North Korea is at least economically integrated into the
regional market, and on the resolution of long running disputes between
Russia and Japan. Development of some oil and gas resources within the
region also depend on China's borders being stabilized. As in the Middle
East, therefore, large energy options depend on larger political issues. The
key questions are:

• How will the evolution of relations between China and its neighbours
  affect the development of resources within the region?
• What scope is there for cooperation between China, Russia, Korea and
  Japan on the possibility of enlarging energy supplies to East Asia by the
  development of east Russian gas?

Nuclear energy

The future of the nuclear industry is also entangled with non-energy events.
Nuclear disarmament creates surpluses of weapons grade plutonium.
Weaker controls in the former Soviet Union create the risk of illegal trade
in plutonium. The attitude of Iraq and North Korea to their obligations
under the Nuclear Non-proliferation Treaty have led some of the main
nuclear-weapons powers to obstruct the acquisition of even civil nuclear
technology by non-nuclear-weapons countries. Even conventional trade in
spent and reprocessed fuel and the storage of spent fuel are thought to be at
risk from theft by international terrorist groups.

The industry has its own specific problems: European and US fears of the
risk of a 'Chernobyl' catastrophe are not matched by willingness to provide
very large resources to make safe or close the older nuclear generating stations in eastern Europe and the former Soviet Union. Private-sector investors
fear the liabilities attached to the risk of leakage of spent fuel in long-term
storage, or other accidents. Governments everywhere are involved in the
nuclear industry more than any other. Developing new designs for 'intrinsi-
cally safe' reactors requires R&D commitments which will not come from
the private sector and may be too large even for individual governments. The
geopolitical international agenda therefore includes:

- agreement on how to control the fuel cycle to prevent weapons development;
- bearing the cost of making existing east European and Russian reactors safer;
- bearing the cost of research and development for safer and more economic reactors in the future.

Climate change

Climate change policy also reflects wider international plays of power and impotence. The arithmetic contains the paradox that most of the concentrations of greenhouse gases now in the upper atmosphere were put there by the fossil-fuel consumption of what are now the world's developed, industrial and relatively rich countries – the signatories to Annex 1 of the UN Convention on Climate Change. This balance is shifting as a result of rapid development (and growing energy consumption) elsewhere, a large part of which – in China and India particularly – is fuelled by CO_2-intensive coal, relatively inefficiently burnt. Within the time span of the climate problem, the balance of responsiblity for the concentration will change. If the governments of Annex 1 countries seriously want to prevent or at least substantially reduce long-term future climate change, they cannot do it alone. They will need not only to develop policies which reduce their own energy demand and shift it towards low CO_2 fuels, but to compensate large energy consumers in the rest of the world for the cost of doing likewise. This necessity puts climate change mitigation firmly in the 'North–South' agenda of global relations between rich and poor.

In addition, there is the possibility that some countries might take strong actions on energy demand and as a result be obliged to protect their economic competitiveness by intervening in the free flow of trade conducted under the hard-won rules of the World Trade Organization. Climate change policies, to which the Annex 1 countries are becoming increasingly committed, therefore add to the international geopolitical agenda the questions of agreement on:

- ways of prioritizing climate change policy among other international issues – for example trade issues;

- ways of differentiating responsibility for actions to limit emissions of greenhouse gases;
- flexible mechanisms to allocate the cost of change, and the risks associated with the probable outcome.

On whose desk? In whose rhetoric?

For every issue on the energy geopolitical agenda, there is at least one telephone line to Washington. There are some such connections to Moscow and Tokyo, but none to Brussels, where governments are distracted with the strain of Europe's own constitutional development. So far, the weakness and complexity of procedures for developing common foreign and security policy mean that there is little European-level influence on these geopolitical issues, though individual governments play some roles: the UK and France in security matters, Germany in relations with Russia and eastern Europe.

The USA

In the world-wide web of policies the US has a full home page:

- The US government promotes free trade and liberalization of investment, and supports private-sector US energy companies in their efforts to develop petroleum supplies around the world.
- The USA is deeply involved in the Middle East: through its security agreements, its pre-positioned military capacity, its support of Gulf state defence forces and the supply of arms – in addition to its commitment to Israel and its efforts in the Middle East peace process.
- The USA is deeply involved with Russia across a vast agenda of relationships: security (including European security and the enlargement of NATO), economic assistance (bilateral and through the IMF and World Bank), and global international relations through the UN Security Council. Dialogue is institutionalized (through the 'Gore–Chernomyrdin' committee) so that issues can be prioritized and coordinated.
- In East Asia, too, the USA is a major player, through its military presence,

its commitments to defend Japan and South Korea, its relationship with Taiwan, and its developing long-term economic and political relationships with China. To the extent that these relations affect energy developments, the USA will have an influence.

- On nuclear energy, the USA is a clear leader in international efforts to limit the risk of nuclear energy development leading to weapons proliferation. It controls, through its leverage over US companies, at least one major potential source of technology.
- Finally, the USA is clearly a major, though not a dominant, player in the international negotiations on climate change policies, and now appears committed to the development of legally binding targets and timetables in this area.

The reach of the USA, and its ability to coordinate its own policies, do not mean that it can decide every issue, in energy or in other matters. The most innovative recent international effort to promote cross-border flows of energy trade and investment was arguably the Energy Charter Treaty which followed the European Energy Charter of 1991, and which the USA has decided not to sign. Russia's voice will be decisive on matters concerning its own resources and powerful in relation to the Caspian. The scope of East Asian cross-border energy projects depends very much on the participation of China and Japan. What happens in the Middle East will in the long run be decided there.

Energy administrations and 'energy policies'

This book has argued that many key issues affecting energy *supply* are under the priority of non-energy 'geopolitical' policies: in the oil-dependent exporters there are priorities of national independence and international rivalry which are constrained by energy opportunities but which also constrain energy actions. In the rapidly growing economies of East Asia, the priority is to support continuing rapid economic development. In many other countries, government interventions in energy are dominated by priorities of foreign and security policy.

Another book could be written arguing that most government interventions affecting energy *demand* (apart from climate change, which is discussed here) are now national policies driven by environmental priorities. Between supply, affected by 'geopolitics', and demand, affected by environmental policies, there is a heap of markets – vibrant and sometimes a little smelly – where the function of balancing demand and supply is performed. That is what old-style energy policies were supposed to do, but that role has ceased to exist in much of the world as governments have retreated from economic management. Talking of such energy policies in today's world seems an unreal and a somewhat nostalgic activity. From the analysis of this report it appears equally unrealistic to treat energy policy as simply an extension for environmental policies: the geopolitical issues matter also.

Energy policy is a taxi

Energy policy, in today's terms, is therefore generally a vehicle which can carry a variety of other policies, but it is a useful vehicle: it matters that it has a competent driver, who knows how to get to the destination the passenger wants, that the cost is shown clearly on the meter, and that the brakes and steering work. In this sense, a good energy policy is like a London taxi. The world's capitals contain many worse alternatives.

Who shares the ride?

The energy–geopolitical links are very diverse: each subject involves a slightly different group of actors and exposure to different sets of non-energy policies. There are numerous examples:

- The G-7 or 'G-7+1' summits, where anything of importance can be linked to anything else.
- A multitude of forums for the Middle East, each with a different focus. The most important – the peace process – has no close energy implications. For the Iraqi sanctions the forum is the Security Council – far removed from energy specifics.

- Bilateral institutions for dialogue with Russia (for example the 'Gore–Chernomyrdin' Committee at the time of writing).
- For European–Russian issues, there is no political forum in which to put energy alongside the wider issues: one success – the Energy Charter Treaty – had a political rather than an energy origin, but has yet to be proved operational.
- In East Asia there is now an Energy Committee of APEC, but Russia – an important potential supplier – is not a member of APEC (and of course, nor are the Middle East countries which are the present main sources of imports to the region).
- For the complex of nuclear questions, the existing international forums and mechanisms are focused on the problems of connections with weapons and not with the question of international cooperation over the civil future of nuclear energy.
- The intergovernmental meetings on climate change attack demand, and seem designed to ignore, rather than solve, the questions of adapting supply except in the very long-term sense of promoting renewable energy. The nuclear option is not discussed.
- The 'producer–consumer dialogue', sponsored by successive groups of energy producing governments and the IEA secretariat, is on the one hand too wide (many governments involved are minor actors in energy and the geopolitics which affect it); on the other hand it is too narrow (because the agenda appears to be about energy, from whose active management many 'consumer' governments have withdrawn, and it is difficult to get the wider issues on the table).
- Last but not least are the markets in which enterprises operate. However grand the project, in almost every country most energy actions will be realized through enterprises developing projects and facilities, and carrying out trade and distribution. More and more, these are likely to be private-sector enterprises, as privatization advances. Both the private and public sectors require the support in the last resort of an increasingly global financial market. Few governments these days can allocate tax revenues to energy subsidies and projects, though there is an unavoidable role for governments, and for cooperation between governments in creating (or destroying) conditions for enterprises and markets to work.

Coordination

In the 'taxi' metaphor, competing drivers and passengers benefit from a framework which reduces the risks of incompetence and the costs of bargaining. For international relations the consequence of complexity is that there is no single forum or process (below the UN Security Council) in which all the energy-related issues could be brought together. Coordination within administrations and between countries with similar interests is essential to achieve results. There is an unusual responsibility on the USA to provide a degree of coherence, sometimes called leadership, because the US administration has, for a variety of reasons, a significant position in every major area of policy and geography in the geopolitics of energy. This gives the USA an unusual opportunity to shape policies in the direction of its own blend of priorities: such are the costs and rewards of being a superpower.

Projects for international cooperation

One general conclusion from this study has been that, in the 'new geopolitics', energy is generally a vehicle for wider policies – foreign and security policies on the supply side and in climate change, other environmental objectives on the demand side. These policies operate in and around markets and the private sector. The analysis showed cases where 'geopolitics' wider than energy would determine or at least shape energy developments. There are also reverse possibilities. Cooperation to achieve and share the benefits of certain major energy 'projects', defined in the widest sense, could contribute to wider cooperation and put constraints on the development of conflicts. Examples are:

- The promotion of stable conditions for international flows of technology and investment in energy supply and transportation: the Energy Charter Treaty may be a beginning.
- Wider and deeper cooperation to reduce the risk of temporary disruptions of energy supplies and manage them when they occur: the broadening of the IEA-type sharing arrangements to include non-member major countries would be an example.

- A multilateral effort to stabilize the transit conditions for Russian energy exports to western Europe and to enable the development of Central Asian oil and gas for world markets.
- Intergovernmental cooperation to develop a framework for the investments necessary to expand potential gas supplies to East Asia, including pipeline gas from eastern Russia.
- Cooperation to address outstanding problems so that the 'nuclear option' for climate-benign energy is not closed for lack of private-sector commitment to research and development.
- Bridging the gap between Annex 1 and other countries in policies towards mitigating the risks of climate change by policies which all countries can accept as fair and practical.

Each of these 'projects' is complex, long-term, and international in the commitments required and the benefits likely to accrue. None of them will progress without support of some kind from the governments directly concerned. The above is a checklist against which the development of the 'new geopolitics of energy' can be measured. The good news is that there are political as well as economic prizes to be won.

References

Adelman, M.A. (1993). 'Modelling World Oil Supply', *The Energy Journal*, Vol. 14, No. 1, pp. 1–32.

Adelman, M.A. (1995). *The Genie Out of the Bottle: World Oil since 1970*, Massachusetts Institute of Technology, Cambridge, MA.

Appert, Olivier (1995). `Enhanced Collaboration in Energy Technology', paper for IEA Third Meeting of Experts from Energy Exporting and Importing Countries, Paris, 12–13 April.

Barnes, Philip (1995). 'Oil Reserves, Concepts, Sources and Interpretations', survey article in the *Journal of Economic Literature*, Vol. 1, No. 1, Oxford Institute of Energy Studies.

Beck, Peter W. (1994). *Prospects and Strategies for Nuclear Power: Global Boon or Dangerous Diversion?*, Royal Institute of International Affairs/Earthscan, London.

British Petroleum (1995). *BP Statistical Review*, London.

Canadian Energy Research Institute (CERI) (1995). *See* Considine and Reinsch (1995).

Considine, Jennifer I. and Reinsch, Anthony E. (1995). *Battle for Market Share: World Oil Market Projects, 1995–2010*, Canadian Energy Research Institute, Calgary.

Crandall, Maureen S. (1994). 'Outlook for Russia: Economics and Energy', paper for MIT Center for Energy and Environmental Policy Research Workshop, US Department of Energy, 28 April.

Davies, Peter (1995). Paper to XVI World Energy Congress, Tokyo.

Demaison, G., Laherre, J. and Perredon, A. (1994). *Undiscovered Petroleum Potential*, Petroconsultants SA, Geneva, Switzerland.

Energy Information Administration (1995). *International Energy Outlook 1995*, EIA/Department of Energy, USA.

European Commission, (1995). *An Energy Policy for the European Union*, White Paper COM(95)682, EEC, Brussels.

Fengqi, Zhou (1995). 'Fuel Quality, Environmental Standards and Costs', paper for IEA Third Meeting of Experts from Energy Exporting and Importing Countries, Paris, 12–13 April.

Garwin, R.L. *et al.*, eds (1994). *Managing the Plutonium Surplus: Applications and Technical Options*, NATO ASI Series/Kluwer Academic Publishers, Dordrecht.

Grubb, Michael *et al.* (1991). *Energy Policies and the Greenhouse Effect, Volume Two: Country Studies and Technical Options*, Royal Institute of International Affairs/Dartmouth, London.

Grubb, Michael (1995). *Renewable Energy Strategies for Europe, Volume 1: Foundations and Context*, Royal Institute of International Affairs/Earthscan, London.

Gustavson, Thane (1989). *Crisis amidst Plenty: Russian Energy Policy under Breshnev and Gorbachev*, Princeton University Press, Princeton, NJ.

Halliday, Fred (1996). *Islam and the Myth of Confrontation*, I.B. Tauris, London.

Hartshorn, J.E. (1993). *Oil Trade: Politics and Prospects*, Cambridge University Press, UK.

Horsnell, P. (1996). *Oil in Asia*, Oxford Institute for Energy Studies.

Horsnell, P. and Mabro, R. (1993). *Oil Markets and Prices: The Brent Market and the Formation of World Oil Prices*, Oxford University Press, UK.

Ikuta, Toyoaki (1995). 'Recent Energy Situations and Energy Policy from now on', *Energy in Japan*, Japan Institute of Energy Economics, Tokyo, November.

Imai, Ryukichi (1995). *Fifty Years after Hiroshima*, Policy Paper 142E, Institute for International Policy Studies, Tokyo, April.

Institut Français du Pétrole (1996). 'Investments in the Oil and Gas Sector', Panorama 96, IFP, Paris.

International Energy Agency (1995a). *Energy Policies of the Russian Federation*, OECD Publications, Paris.

International Energy Agency (1995b). *Middle East Oil and Gas*, OECD Publications, Paris.

International Energy Agency (1995c). *The Natural Gas Security Study*, OECD Publications, Paris.

International Energy Agency (1995d). *North Sea Oil Supply: The Expected*

Peak Recedes Again, OECD Publications, Paris.

International Energy Agency (1995e). *World Energy Outlook*, OECD Publications, Paris.

International Energy Agency (1996). *Oil Market Report* (various issues).

Japan Institute of Energy Economics (1995). *Demand and Supply Outlook for East Asia*, JIEE, Tokyo.

Jennings, J.S. (1995). 'Preparing for our Second Century', address to the Oil and Money Conference, London, 2 November.

Kryukov, Valery and Moe, Arild (1996). *The New Russian Corporatism? A Case Study of Gazprom*, Post-Soviet Business Forum, Royal Institute of International Affairs, London.

Lynch, Michael C. (1995). 'The Analysis and Forecasting of Petroleum Supply: Sources of Error and Bias', presentation for Conference on 'Energy Outlook after 2000', Boulder, CO, April.

Masters, Charles D., Attanasi, Emil D. and Root, David H. (1994). 'World Petroleum Assessment and Analysis', Proceedings of the 14th World Petroleum Conference, John Wiley & Sons, New York, USA.

Mitchell, John V. (1994a). *An Oil Agenda for Europe*, Royal Institute of International Affairs, London.

Mitchell, John V. (1994b). 'Oil Production outside OPEC and the Former Soviet Union: A Model Applied to the US and UK', *The Energy Journal*, Vol. 15, Special Issue, International Association of Energy Economists.

Odell, P. (1980). *The Future of Oil*, Kogan Page, London.

Paik, Keun-Wook (1995). *Gas and Oil in Northeast Asia: Policies, Projects and Prospects*, Royal Institute of International Affairs, London.

Petroleum Economist (1994). Special Report: *Gas in the Former Soviet Union*, September.

Rase, Glenn (1995). 'A Washington Perspective on Caspian Oil and Gas and the Pipeline Options', paper presented at the Conference on 'Oil and Caviar in the Caspian', School of Oriental and African Studies, University of London, 24–25 February.

Roberts, John (1996). *Caspian Pipelines*, Former Soviet South project, Royal Institute of International Affairs, London.

Rodwell, E. *et al.* (1996). *A Review of the Economic Potential of Plutonium in spent Fuel*, EPRI Report TR-106072, The Electric Power Research

Institute, Palo Alto, CA, February.

Schipper, Lee and Meyers, Stephen (1992). *Energy Efficiency and Human Activity: Past Trends and Future Prospects*, Cambridge University Press/Stockholm Environment Institute.

Schipper, Lee and Meyers, Stephen (1993). 'Using Scenarios to Explore Future Energy Demand in Industrialised Countries', *Energy Policy*, Vol. 21, No. 3, March, Butterworth-Heinemann.

Seaborg, Glen, *et al.* (1995). *Protection and Management of Plutonium*, American Nuclear Society, Special Panel Report.

Siddiqui, Toufiq A. (1994). 'Implications for Energy and Climate Change Policies of Using Purchasing-Power-Parity-based GDP', *Energy*, Vol. 19, No. 9, Pergamon.

Stern, Jonathan (1995). *Russian Natural Gas 'Bubble': Consequences for European Gas Markets*, Royal Institute of International Affairs, London.

Stewart, Alex (1995). *Energy Security in North Asia: The Opportunity for Russian Gas*, ING Barings, Global Sector Research, London.

Streifel, Shane S. (1995). 'Review and Outlook for the World Oil Market', IBRD/World Bank, Washington, DC.

Uibopuu, Henn-Jüri (1995). 'The Caspian Sea: A Tangle of Legal Problems', *The World Today*, RIIA, Vol. 51, No. 6 (June).

Weaver, Robert (1994), 'Financial and Capital Requirements', Eighth International Energy Conference on 'Energy Structures in Energy Industries', Royal Institute of International Affairs, 6–7 December 1993.

World Bank (1993). *Energy Efficiency and Conservation in the Developing World*, World Bank, Washington, DC.

World Bank (1995). *World Development Report 1995*, Oxford University Press.

World Commission on Environment and Development (1987). *Our Common Future,* Oxford University Press, Oxford.

Yergin, Daniel and Gustavson, Thane (1993). *Russia 2010 and What it Means for the Rest of the World: The CERA report*, Random House, New York.